Pastor Darren Farmer

BROKEN

Restoration
For God's
Wounded

© 2009 Pastor Darren Farmer
All rights reserved.
Printed in the United States of America
ISBN: 1-4392-5621-7
EAN13: 9781439256213
Visit www.booksurge.com to order additional copies.

Acknowledgements

I wish to express my deepest appreciation to my wife, Amanda, for her constant love, support and encouragement during the process of writing this book and her willingness to allow me to be honest, not only with the struggles and mistakes I made, but allowing me to write openly about the trials we faced together. Today we can both rejoice in the grace and full restoration that God has brought into our lives.

To Katelynn, Brooklynn and Connor for giving up hours on the computer, so I could write. For all the inspiration they have given me and for allowing me to love them unconditionally.

To my Parents, Margaret and Roy Farmer, my Sister Mandy and her husband Jon and my brother Nigel and His wife Ester, for their continuous love, support and belief in us and in the ministry God has called us to.

To Robin Hamilton and Pastor Chris Rouse for the many hours of reading, editing and enthusiasm for this project.

My utmost praise must go to my Lord and Savior, Jesus Christ, who called me despite my weaknesses, and restored me according to His truth and unfathomable grace.

Contents

BROKEN

Introduction

It's an awesome feeling to stand on top of Cadillac Mountain in Acadia National Park, in "Vacation Land", Maine. This mountain is the highest point along the North Atlantic seaboard and the first place to see sunrise in the USA. It's amazing to stand there excited and in anticipation as you wait for the darkness of the night to pass away, knowing that you are among the first people that day, to see the sun rise.

Looking in the sky you see the wonder of the heavens, as magical colors fill the horizon, the darkness gives way to light, the islands and ocean come into view. The lights in homes below begin to turn on as the town of Bar Harbor wakes. You realize today is a new day!!!

Many off us have experienced darkness and the feeling of hopelessness in our lives. Life throws a curve ball and suddenly we are faced with challenges that we never thought we would face. We feel overtaken by life's surprises and while we are in the midst of the problems we wonder if there will ever be an end to the pain. Is there a light at the end of the tunnel? Is there any hope of a way through the wilderness we have entered?

This is a midnight experience, where, like Jacob, we wrestle with God as we try to find a way back to blessings and happiness. The night is long and the struggle drains us of energy and life. Tired and perplexed we cling on to God with our fingertips in hope that we can make it through. Then suddenly, the night breaks and it's a new day. Everything that has gone before is finished and the hope of a new beginning is upon us. The despair and hopelessness is gone and the life of God fills us again as blessings are restored in our lives. (Gen 32:22-30)

We all dream of a perfect church and yet our desire is impossible as the church is full of imperfect people who make mistakes or are affected by other people's decisions. Many people in the church are hurting and at times the leaders are unsympathetic towards those individuals as they struggle to know how to reach out to them. Jesus has the answer and as the Healer, He reaches out not only to the unbeliever but also to the lost and hurting church

Through the pages of this book I want to open my life to you as a real experience of a minister who had the "world at his feet" yet suddenly I found myself facing divorce, failure and many questions about the future. As God reached out to heal me, so He wants to reach out and heal you, His people. He wants to bring us through our "Night" experience into the breaking of the dawn, that we may marvel at the new day God has created for us and welcome a new beginning.

Chapter 1
WINNERS

The gun goes off, the race is underway. The "Golden Mile" track and field event is a middle distance run with many twists and turns, lasting less than four minutes. The early leaders are pushing hard as the rest of the pack settles into their stride. Few changes occur early in the race as the athletes wait for the flag that signals the final lap. As their legs start to burn and fatigue sets in, they know they have to dig deep, kick harder and increase the pace if they are to reach the finish line first.

They pass the flag and the pack burst into life as the runners push for the front. Suddenly there's a scream of pain as the favorite stumbles and hits the ground hard, and from nowhere, the newcomer, with youth and belief in his heart, sees his opportunity. He picks up his pace, passing those in front of him and with a sprint, reaches the finished line. He raises his arms in victory and gets ready for his lap of honor. There is a new hero, a new champion and new headlines will be written within hours.

Everyone loves a winner regardless if it's an athlete, singer, actor, business guru or preacher. We want to see people succeed. Well, for a week or two, and then we become obsessed about their lives, their interests, their latest achievements and we predict how long they will last and what they will do next. With one side of our mouth we sing their praise while we watch the news and read the tabloids to see the mistakes they are making.

News is made by great winners and achievers but more interesting news is made when those achievers fail, fall, stumble and before long they are out of the game!! What is it about the heart of man that wants people to both succeed and fail? The reality is we all want to be winners but we also realize that we all have things we struggle with and we know in one way or another we will fail.

It becomes easier for us to identify with people that struggle than people who succeed! We cannot run or hide from our imperfections. Like me, at some point in our life they will find us out. The question isn't, will we fail or make mistakes, but what will we do after we make mistakes?

The Bible is full of winners, but winners who made mistakes and failed. Great kings, Judges and Apostles who hear the call of God and start off well yet at some point they take their eye off the goal, and exchange holiness for fleshly desires. They commit murder or acts of adultery; they scheme and try to lie their way out of the mess. They become arrogant, self-seeking, proud, boastful, and angry. One great Apostle rejected his friendship with Jesus yet God, in His grace, did not let him go or give up on him. *(John 18:15-18, John 21)*

Jesus is not like man, who waits for people to fall to declare, "I told you so" and with a simple statement, writes the individual off. Jesus has a plan in place to bring restoration. He knows we will fail, stumble and fall. This plan was revealed a number of times in the life of Peter.

The first time we see this is when Peter wanted to walk on water like his Master. With great confidence, Peter stepped out of the boat and made his way to Jesus. In the midst of his journey, he took his eyes off Jesus turning his attention to the storm and he began to sink. You can imagine the scene, as the other disciples looked on, perhaps even thinking, "I knew it was a bad idea, I tried to stop him". Jesus had one thing in mind – restoration. Immediately, He responded with grace as He reached out his hand and grabbed hold of Peter, restoring him to a place of security, standing next to Him on the water. *(Matthew 14:22-33)* The scripture does not expound on the journey back to the boat but there must have been one. If Peter got out of the boat and walked a little way to Jesus, then he would have had to walk back to the boat, but this time they walked together.

We can only imagine the feeling of joy Peter must have experienced, after failing, when he suddenly found himself walking on the water with Jesus. How glorious! All the other disciples could do was to look on and see this great miraculous event.

The great plan that God has for us is a plan of restoration. This is a word that God shouts out to those Christian believers who have failed, lied, schemed, and denied Him. They committed adultery, had sexual relationships outside of marriage or aborted a child. The list can go on and on, yet God still wants to restore you. This is not an excuse to sin and do what you like, it's a place of true repentance and realization that God still has a plan for your life.

Paul in his letter to the churches in Galatia *(Galatians 6:1)* exhorts those who are "spiritual" to restore those who have fallen. If he were writing this today, he would be addressing pastors, youth leaders, home group leaders and encouraging them to restore those who have sinned. Often the church is quick to pass judgment, as it strives for holiness yet slow to show the heart and ministry of Jesus in reaching out a healing hand to the hurting, bleeding, self-condemned believer, who needs support to get back on track.

It is difficult for the church to balance the standards of God and His holiness with His grace and mercy. John, the apostle of love, summed it up when he wrote in John 1:14 that Jesus was *"full (lacking nothing) of grace and truth"* Two words that seem to be at odds with each other. How do they co-exist in the same world or church?

God's truth is His standard yet God knows we are not able to attain this standard, as we are not God or perfect. We live in a fallen world and at times we follow the desires of the flesh. It's in these moments when we miss the mark that we need to repent and trust God to extend His grace to us. As believers we need to aim for truth, yet when we fall short, hold tight to grace!

Again as leaders, we find it's easy when we are dealing with an un-believer's many flaws, yet when they make the decision to follow Jesus, he or she will experience God's grace. It's a new start, they are forgiven! They have great opportunities in front of them. Why do we struggle to reflect the same grace when a believer makes a mistake thinking they should know better? For leaders or pastors to act differently towards the struggling saint, is to say that God has changed. We are saying that He is the God of grace to the un-believer and the God of truth to the believer, when the scripture is clear that He is the God of grace and truth all the time. God is steadfast in His character. He never changes and continues to teach us truth, reaching out to us in grace.

The Apostle Paul grabs hold of this issue passionately encourag-ing the *"spiritual to restore those who have fallen"*. *(Galatians 6:1)* This is a great word because it not only expresses the thought of forgiveness but also stretches us to a place where we work with the person who has sinned. It encourages us to strengthen them, adjust them, re-position and realign them until they are healed and fully restored. To restore a person, scripturally speaking, takes us beyond our human thinking. When we imagine an athlete, pop star or preacher that has fallen we speak of their restoration, hoping they will make a come back. But God's restoration is so complete that He brings them beyond their previous level of functioning into their full potential by His grace.

When the scripture speaks of restoration it reflects the heart of God, which not only wants to restore us to the position from which we fell but bring us to a place of greater influence and sig-nificance. We will see this later as we look at how Jesus restored Peter from a place of rejecting Him, to experiencing grace and being restored not only to the team of disciples but becoming the leader of the early Church.

You may have made mistakes or fallen from a position of leader-ship, the heart of God is to restore you and increase you!

The rest of this book will tell my story of a great beginning, the painful journey of a failed marriage and ministry and the unbelievable grace of God who reached out and restored me as a person, family man and minister of the Gospel. I have endeavored to reveal to you the "good, bad and the ugly". We can only fully understand God's restoration if we understand where we have fallen from. The place we fell from becomes the minimum or the benchmark to which God wants to restore us. If that's not true it's not restoration, just partial restoration which is not the heart of God.

Early Years

November 5, 1971, its bonfire night in England. It is a strange time of year when the British people celebrate the failed gunpowder plot on the House of Parliament by Guy Fawkes in 1605. Yes, every year on November 5, this intelligent nation abandons their books and reserved nature. They stand outside on a cold night, wrapped in winter gear making stuffed newspaper dummies, replicating Mr. Guys Fawkes. These are strategically placed on the top of the fire and everyone watches him burst into flames. During this time hundreds of fireworks are released into the heavens with all the sights, colors, whooshes and explosions that make for a great display.

It was to this wonderful sound that I was born in Birmingham, England. There were no angels singing (that could be heard) and there were no prophets in the room to declare the great things I would do for the Kingdom of God. There were two very devoted parents who would prove to be great role models in the years to come.

Why is this important? Whenever a person sins or fails, the experts want to examine the person's childhood or their parents. We are always looking for a reason why we failed. If you go through a divorce like myself, people want to know if your parent's were divorced. This gives them a so-called idea of why your marriage may have failed. Even though I acknowledge that we are strongly influenced by our parents' example to us, they can never be the reason why we fail. To use this as an excuse causes us to take our eyes off the problems that exist in our own lives or character. As long as we try to blame others, we will never truly repent of the things we have done and we will fail to find the real answers to our problems, restricting us from moving forward.

This is similar to the actions of King Saul. God gave him very specific instructions to wait for Samuel, the prophet, to burn the offering *(1 Samuel 10:8)*. When the children of Israel came under attack from the Philistines, King Saul acted out of his fear of failure and listened to the voice of the people and brought the offering. This was in direct disobedience to God. When the Prophet Samuel arrived he questioned the king's action. Saul became defensive and blamed others declaring, *"I felt compelled by the people."* He failed to accept his own sins and faults. This caused him to lose the kingdom *(1 Samuel 13)*. The only person that can stop us from being restored is ourselves. This happens when we refuse to accept our faults and deal with them. I am sure we have all blamed someone else at some point for our mistakes. The key is that we need to recognize our mistakes, own them and deal with them. Until we face them head-on, they will continue to burden us and restrict us from moving forward.

It may also become a stronghold of the enemy in our minds, that if we failed in our marriage so will our children. We may forever live in guilt and fear that their marriages will fail because of the bad examples we have provided. If they should fail, we struggle to forgive ourselves. The reality is that every person has free will and while divorce is not a good example, Christ in their heart can lead them into great relationships and sound marriages. If this were not true, we are saying that our example is more powerful than God in their lives. We know God to be all-powerful. In dealing with our sins, we have to accept the grace of God and move on, endeavoring to give a better example in the future.

I believe it's more important to be real with our children and talk about both our success and failures. This is what God did with us, when He inspired the writing of His Word. He shows people in their glorious and not so glorious actions. We need to let children see the full picture in hopes that through Christ, they may avoid the pit holes, we fell through.

I grew up in a wonderful home with my sister Mandy, brother Nigel, and two very supportive parents, who continue to be as devoted to each other as they are to us. Over the years, they have been great encouragers. Even though we were not a church going family during my early childhood my parents instilled the belief that we could achieve anything we wanted.

Ours was a typical sport-crazy family. Well, I speak for my father, brother and myself. The girls did "girly things." My parents worked hard. Sometime they worked two jobs at a time to make ends meet. They never took time off when they were sick or because they wanted a rest. They had a great work ethic realizing that what they put in they would get out. They didn't have the best jobs, that paid the most money but I can honestly say that I never heard them complain about going to work. We always had a great Christmas and a family vacation every year. In those early years, we never had a weekly allowance, but we knew when it was payday because Dad never failed to come home with a bar of chocolate for each of us. It doesn't sound much in today's world, but back then it was everything.

My parents needed to work, which meant that we all had to help around the house. At a young age we all could cook, well, with the exception of my sister. Being the oldest, she knew the art of delegation. I became the cook and Mandy stayed out of the kitchen. Despite this, in later years she would become quite the cook! We could all iron and take care of things that needed to be done. This didn't mean we had clean bedrooms, we were still kids, but we knew how to look after ourselves.

My parents' work ethic inspired me, and taught me that if I wanted nice things I had to go and get money. From the age of thirteen, I was delivering newspapers and working in the local store. I wanted the latest sports wear, and I knew how to get it – work hard. It was their inspiration that gave me the understanding that, if I wanted something badly enough, I could find an honest way to get it. Their example made me a winner!

Once the day was finished and mom and dad were home, it was all about family. We would eat together, watch TV together and dad would take us to the park for yet another game of soccer. Everyday I heard my parents tell us that they loved us as they showered us with hugs and kisses. We knew that if we made mistakes they would correct us but soon after we would be showered with love. Their love has never changed. They have always been there to support and encourage us even when we made big mistakes. You can see from my family that they laid a great foundation for success and their example was inspiring and empowering.

Sports were my life, especially soccer. Every minute I had I was practicing, playing, or finding a group of people to play the beautiful game. At a young age I found inspiration from sport heroes. In addition to these sporting heroes, I loved to see people who were considered underdogs succeed and prove that anyone could do anything.

As a student I went to a multicultural school with many nationalities. This would prove to be an inspiration to me once I became a Christian. My desire to get to school every morning was to play sport. I had no real interest in education and my attitude caused me to suffer in class. I didn't read well and I didn't like the sound of my accent. If you have been to Birmingham, England, you know it is very strong. This caused me to feel stupid so I didn't like talking to people. At that point in my life I had no desire for education. My only desire was to play soccer and make it big!! I always thought big and although I never made it in the world of sport, due to my passion to preach, sport gave me the ability to see beyond my weakness of a lack of education, and take advantage of my strengths, a winning spirit.

When I was growing up I was privileged to see the like's of Lady Thatcher take on a man's world of politics' and against the odds she become the first, and to date, the only woman Prime Minister. She was known as the "Iron Lady" and with great tenacity she led the country from 1979 to 1990 in the midst of riots, strikes, poverty and the Falkland War with Argentina. She was a winner. Regardless of the distance between main land Britain and the Falkland Islands, she would not roll over and give up what she believed belonged to the British people who lived on that island. With great strategic maneuverings and motivation, she led the country to victory. Lady Thatcher's example and determination to succeed in a man's world, was something that God used to inspire me in the belief that I could succeed in whatever I chose to do, especially if God was calling me. I believe God loves to take the weak things of this world to confound the wise. *(1 Corinthians 1:27)*

I was not the easiest child to live with. I was very determined, self willed and at times stubborn. On the outside I was strong and hard but on the inside I was struggling. The questions of life always caused me great fear. What was life all about? What happens when we die? Is there a God? What about sickness, disease and worst of all what would happen if we suffered a nuclear strike from Russia? Back in the seventies and eighties this was what everyone was talking about in school and I was waiting for the bomb to drop! These questions were in my head all the time and they kept me awake at night. I would go to bed, sleep for a few hours and then I was up thinking about the questions of life. Mom and dad were there to comfort me and even though they tried to answer my questions, at that time they didn't have the answers I was looking for.

Fear grew in my heart and I didn't know what to do with it. The church didn't help me either. I remember joining a church club and going for about six weeks before I had to stop because part of the conditions for being in the club was going to church on a Sunday. I would go but the questions and fear I had grew worse. It seemed to create more questions and less answers. It made me think about God and life more than at other times and I left more confused. The strange thing was even then, when my whole purpose in life was to play soccer professionally, there was the tiny thought that kept coming into my mind. "One day you will be a preacher"

Salvation

On December 13, 1986 there was a knock on the door and my friend stood there with mischief in his eyes as he informed me that a weird church group was on the street corner, playing music and talking about God. Well, with my hatred for church, we decided we would cause some trouble and before long they would be out of the way. This was our territory, and no church group would be able to invade it!

Within minutes we were standing in front of this group of people, ready to unload trouble! Yet in those moments something got hold of me and I was transfixed. All the life questions filled my mind. The thought that one day I would be a preacher infiltrated my heart and all I could do was listen. When the preacher made his way towards me, he fixed his eyes on mine. I knew it was time to get out of there, but I couldn't. He started asking me questions about my heart, life, sin and death!

I thought, "Ok, it's time for real questions; let's see if he can deal with mine!" I started talking about the things that troubled me. As quickly as I asked the questions he had answers that made sense. Within a short period of time, he was asking me if I wanted to know Jesus and invite him into my heart. I knew that this was it and there on that cold winter's day, I closed my eyes and made a commitment to Christ. Suddenly, as I prayed the sinner's prayer, the preacher, asked the Holy Spirit to confirm my salvation. Wow! My body felt light as though a weight was lifted off me. I could feel the presence of God. The fear that had tormented my mind was lifted from me and I knew that I knew there was a God!

I honestly cannot remember what happened to my friend that day. I don't remember him leaving, or any other conversation we had. I was just elated, my heart was full of joy and I couldn't wait to get home and tell my parents I was going to church! You can image their shock and at the same time, fear. "What has he gotten himself into this time?"

The next day, I went to church and a great journey of discovery started. This was a new church that would become one of the leading churches in our city. The organ had been replaced by a worship team that looked like a rock band. The members had long hair, leather jackets and they played electric guitars. This was not like any church I had been to before... it rocked!!

Woodgate Church was located in a suburb of Birmingham. At that time, it was a small church, but it would soon see an explosion of growth. Even though it was non-denominational, its leaders had been greatly influenced by John Wimber and the Vineyard movement. The church had great praise and worship. The Word of God was delivered with authority and like John Wimber, the church moved in the supernatural. It was normal for the church to pray for the sick and see great miracles take place. I'm not just talking about headaches and heart burn being healed but deaf ears were opened, eye sight was restored, broken bones made new and cancer driven out of people bodies. This church was a place that you could experience the gifts and the ministry of the Holy Spirit. I wasted no time; I wanted all that was offered. Like those I watched. I wanted to be filled with the Holy Spirit and minister to the sick.

Mini –Revival

When we read the book of Acts, we see the Apostle Paul experienced a miraculous salvation. He was filled with the Holy Spirit and "immediately he preached Christ" *(Acts 9:20)* Like Paul, no one told me to start preaching, I just couldn't help myself. What I was experiencing in church, I wanted other people to experience. They needed to know about Jesus Christ and the freedom He brings. I had to preach about Jesus every opportunity I could. Within weeks, my brother, then my mom and sister made decisions for Jesus. It would be a few more years before my dad made that decision but it was clear that something was happening in our home.

Acts 4:31 speaks of a time when the Holy Spirit came upon the early church and they were filled with boldness and they preached the gospel with power. I didn't know what was happening to me but on Sunday's I would be filled with the Holy Spirit and on a Monday I was ready to preach. Great boldness came upon me. My fear of speaking to people disappeared. I went from preaching to my brother and sister, to preaching to my cousins, school friends, neighbors and whoever else would listen to me.

On one occasion, I remember my Mother telling me that her sister had been struggling for some time with severe pain in her neck. She had been to a number of doctors, tried various medications and there had been no improvement. I was quick to tell my mom, that all we needed to do was pray for her and God would heal her. To my surprise my mother believed what I said and before I knew it, my Aunty Betty was in the house waiting for me to pray for her. "Well, let's give it a go," I thought. I closed my eyes and commanded the sickness to loose her body. Immediately the Spirit of God fell on her, she fell back into the chair (we had no one to catch her) and within minutes we were all shocked to hear her tell us the pain had gone! Jesus had healed her and she remains healed to this day.

This was the start of reaching out to anyone who was sick. I realized that we needed to reach out to people on a Monday the same way the church did on a Sunday. Within a few months I was inviting people to my parent's home and we would have "church" in the living room. Twenty-five people would be jammed into the small room to worship together. Every time we met, we prayed for each other, used the gifts of the Spirit, cast out demons and prayed for the sick. We saw many miracles happen and many people became Christians. I didn't understand the theology to do with ministry, I just knew God could do it, so I let Him. We never thought of this gathering as a new church, we were just doing what we were told to do on a Sunday. Whenever there was a church meeting we were there to support and help as much as we could. Once we left, we would just continue this move of God in my parents' home, on the streets or anywhere people would listen.

Calling

During this time of outpouring, God was also doing something in my heart concerning His call upon my Life. I had been a Christian for about two weeks, when I first heard God speak to me about preaching. I was convinced He would send me to the ends of the earth to minister. There was also something very specific I heard God say to me and it caught my attention. I heard Him say that, "I would succeed where Moses failed."

This caused some questions, because I didn't know who Moses was and I didn't know how he had failed. When I asked one or two people at church they told me about Moses but they didn't understand how Moses failed. He had been a great leader who guided Israel out of captivity and to the edge of the Promised Land. That was what drove me to getting hold of the Bible myself. From that point, I started reading it everyday, every night and every spare minute I had. I couldn't put the Bible down. My reading ability suddenly started to improve. Then one evening as I was reading, I came to the place that spoke about Moses. Excitement rose in my heart, as I knew this was what God was saying to me. Moses had been in Egypt as the adopted son of Pharaoh for 40 years and in his attempt to protect a fellow Israelite, he killed a man. With great fear Moses ran for his life and escaped into the wilderness. After another 40 years, God called Moses out of the wilderness and spoke to him through a burning bush, calling him to lead Israel out of Egypt. *(Exodus 1-3)*

You would think this supernatural experience would have Moses dancing with joy and unstoppable in his call to lead the Children of Israel out of captivity. However, Moses stumbled over an area of fear. It wasn't past sin or the strength of Egypt's army that caused his hesitation to answer God's call - it was the way he spoke! He saw his weakness and he didn't have confidence in his own ability. He tried to defend himself by telling God that *"I am not eloquent… but slow of tongue" (Exodus 4:10)* God quickly responded and encouraged Moses. He told him that He would be with him. Moses still refused to speak. In the end God chose Aaron, Moses brother as his mouthpiece to speaking to the Children of Israel. It was in the area of communication that Moses failed as a leader. I now understood what God was saying to me. He knew that I too hated speaking to people because I didn't think I was eloquent.

When I read this, I decided that I would never let my fear of speaking to people get in the way of what God wanted me to do. I was ready and willing to do whatever He asked of me. This scripture was not only a great influence in my early years as a Christian, but it has continued to influence me throughout my ministry and into my restoration. God's Living Word was true then and it is true now. God continues to look for obedience. We must continue to hold on to the promises and words God gives us, as they will strengthen us throughout our life and ministry.

When we go through an area of failure all our weaknesses seem to surface causing us to question our capabilities. It is in these times that we must hold onto the Word that God spoken into our hearts. What God has spoken, will come to pass. There may be a pause in God's plan when we make decisions that are contrary to His will. We may endure a wilderness season like Moses, but the word that God has spoken to us remain true and God remains faithful to His promises.

Doors start to open

Due to my childhood experience and my parents' example, I realized that nothing would be achieved if I didn't do something with the things God had spoken to me about. No matter how many dreams, aspirations or words from God I had received, I had to do be willing to step out in faith and take action. With this in mind, I set my heart to serve the church. Anything I could do to help the church grow, I would do. I made sure I was first at church to help set up and the last to leave. I took the responsibility of cleaning the church seriously. At the end of one of the services, a member of the congregation came over to me and started to prophecy that "as I was faithful in little God would give me much". Then God spoke into my heart and told me I was going on a mission trip with the church.

I remember going home and talking with my sister about it. She was quick to tell me that I needed to forget about it, after all, I was only sixteen. It would be something in the future. That night when I returned to the church, the pastor started to tell me about a mission trip the church was taking to Italy. I don't remember the message he preached that night, but I remember listening intensely to the details about the mission trip and hoped they would ask me to go. After the service, the minister asked me to join a team of eight people going to Sicily.

The mission trip was a wonderful time of ministry. We prayed for the sick and saw many miracles. I came back from Sicily with a fire burning like never before and a desire to preach and to take the Word of God anywhere He desired. In the weeks and months to come I would hound the leaders for opportunities to preach and before long I was ministering in the Youth Club and home group. God had started a great work and everyone who came in contact with me knew that I was committed to preaching the Word of God and ministering to the sick.

It's easy to look back at your church experiences and see the way the church failed. I am sure that in every church you have attended, there have been some failures and mistakes. We need to balance these times with the good things that took place. I will always be indebted to Woodgate Church and its ministers for the many opportunities they gave me. They did not look at my age but rather recognized the gift and tried to develop it in the best way they knew.

Who is she?

It was during this year that Laura (not her actual name) started attending the church with her friend. They would come just before the service started and leave as soon as it finished. She was tall, thin and she had long "rocker style" hair. She intrigued me. I made it my goal to find out who she was and to get her involved with the young people in the church because that meant she would spend time with me!

After a couple of months of getting to know Laura, God spoke to me and told me that I would marry her. Laura was less keen when I told her and when I announced my intentions. Yes, you read it right, I didn't ask her and I wasn't dating her at the time, I just told her what I believed! As you can imagine, I set myself up for rejection, and for the next few months as I continued my pursuit, she would continue to tell me that she was not interested. Then the day came that she realized she was interested, and we started dating. We were together for three years before we married in May 1991. I was nineteen and Laura was twenty-three. Our life together was before us and we thought it would be forever.

Why is this important when the majority of this book is talking about failure and restoration? I want to stress that God spoke to me and in time also to Laura about getting married. Not only did we want to be together, we believed that God was leading us and we would be obedient to His call. This is a major issue in restoration as many Christians believe God has spoken to them concerning their partner. What you do with that foundational belief when you find yourself in a position of separation or divorce? We explore this issue and the challenges I faced with this foundational belief in another chapter.

From that point on, both Laura and I worked together in partnership in the church looking forward to the ministry God had for us. Over the next few years we found ourselves in the center of church life and ministry. We worked with the youth, ran a home group, oversaw the Children's ministry and took every opportunity presented to help people. It was a very busy and fun time. We both worked full-time jobs and ministered during the evenings. We were consumed with church life and ministry.

During this time we also enrolled in a part-time Bible School (called the School of the Prophets) where we worked hard to achieve the best grades. This was very important to me because I had never had a desire to do well at school and as a result achieved little. The Bible School was different. The kingdom of God was my passion and I was determined to put as much time into studying as was required. I wanted to do well and achieve all that God had called me to do. The school was an intricate part of the church. We believed that if you were to achieve anything in the ministry you had to do well in Bible School. During this time, my love and knowledge of the Word grew. After three years I graduated with distinction holding an average grade of 93% in my exams. It seemed at this time and in the years to come, that all I put my hands to, God blessed.

Call to Bristol

As we continued to be dedicated to Woodgate Church, we knew that God had called us to plant churches. He had given us a vision based on Ephesians 4:11 which says:

> *"And He himself gave some to be apostles, some prophets, some evangelists, and some pastors and teachers for the equipping of the saints for the work of the ministry, for the edifying of the body of Christ."*

We knew that we were called to plant churches that equipped the congregation to do the works of Christ, so they could minister to the world. The churches were team-based, not structured with the minister in total control dictating everything. The leaders of these new churches worked within the five-fold ministry gifts of apostles, prophets, pastors, teachers and evangelists. Together they modeled and released the church into greater works.

I remember going to work every morning asking God "Is it time?" With each question came the response," Be patient, keep serving, and stay committed," until the summer of 1994. I was working for a manufacturing company in Birmingham, selling products to the construction industry. One morning as I was driving my vehicle, asking God "when?" I heard Him speak to me with an audible voice. Everything else became silent and all I could hear was the voice of God. I had heard God speak to me on many occasions but this was different. It wasn't just in my spirit, or a feeling, or thought in my head; I could hear God through my natural ears. When God spoke, He gave me specific instructions to plant a church and that the doors of the church were to open on the 5th of September, 1995. I knew this was God and we would work towards this date. During that time in my life I was consumed with the Old Testament. I studied and saw that when the tabernacle was built, God gave the specific details to Moses. This gave me faith that God could and would speak to me in the same detail. He did not disappoint me. God gave me a time frame and strategy, but He did not tell me the location for the church for several months.

This was a step of faith for Laura and me. God had clearly spoken but how do you prepare when you don't know where you're going? We started to pray and before long my brother Nigel joined us in prayer and committed his life to the mission of planting churches.

Telling the church leaders was "fun"! They believed that we had been called by God to be sent out, but they had difficulty believing that this was the right time without knowing where we were to start the church. The fact that I was twenty-two and Laura was twenty-six was also a concern. Although they had given us many responsibilities and ministry opportunities, the elders believed that leading a church was different. We lived in a country where you did not lead a church until you were older. We sometimes forget that Jesus was a young man when He started his ministry and many of the disciples were in their twenties. As with other battles we faced, opposition moved us into prayer and taking a stand on the Word of God. If God could call and use the Prophet Jeremiah in his youth, then the same God could call and use us. *(Jeremiah 1:1-10)* God's Word gave us faith that we could overcome every obstacle and succeed. In time, through much prayer, God revealed to Laura, Nigel and myself that the destination for the new church was Bristol and together we followed God's plan. In May 1995, the church we had been attending, laid hands on us, prayed over us and sent us to start this new work. We had a few months to find a home, jobs and a place for the church to meet. Then we started to tell people we were there!

This seemed impossible for us, but we knew that we were in the plan of God. We knew that He would open doors and they started to open quickly! We were soon in a new home, had new jobs and we found a school hall for the church to meet in. We booked the facility on a long-term contract with no other members. We acted on the start date that God had spoken. With a deadline before us we began knocking on doors, telling people about Jesus and the new church that was opening in their area. By that Sunday in September 1995, I was very nervous. We had knocked on two thousand doors, delivered five thousand flyers and I had preached my first sermon to myself many times. Now I wondered if anyone would turn up? The service was to start at 6PM. At 5.30PM, with the exception of a few friends, from Birmingham there was little sight of anyone else. The mental battle began. I knew God had spoken about the time but what if we had the wrong place? Within the next thirty minutes, people came from nowhere. At 6PM, the service started with forty-two people! We worshiped God, preached, the Word and prayed for the sick. The church was born!

Every week we saw the church grow as we continued to encourage the congregation to bring their family and friends. From the first Sunday, we started training people to do the works of Christ, using the gifts of the Spirit, praying for individuals. The power of God was evident as people were filled with the Holy Spirit. Individuals were healed and many people made decision for Christ. Within a couple of years, the church numbered three hundred people. We needed our own building and there was one for sale! An old, single screen cinema that could seat nine hundred people was located one mile from the school hall where we had been meeting. It appeared to be the ideal place and the church started to pray.

I decided that it was time to see the bank manager and ask for the money to purchase this wonderful building. I thought the meeting was going well until he gave me his decision. He told me to "lower my sights and find something smaller". I left his office with a righteous anger, and drove to the building, declaring that it would be ours! Within a few months the building sold, but not to us! How could this be? God had spoken to us! Again, I went to the building and declared that it was ours. The church started to pray again and we started taking special offerings for that building. We believed that God had spoken to us and that He would be faithful in providing us with this building.

To our great amazement and joy, the sale of the building fell through and it went on the market again. When I returned to the bank, I was armed with statistics and figures to show the bank manger how we could afford this building without "lowering our sights!" I was surprised to find the old bank manager had gone and a new manager had taken the position that was young and eager to help organizations in the community. Our prayers had been answered! The loan was approved and we started to move in.

From one church to churches

With all the great things God was doing in our lives, it was hard to hold back. We just wanted to push forward and increase the Kingdom of God. We wanted to start more churches with the same team mentality but we didn't have the pastors to do it. What would we do? At this point, God placed a desire in my heart to start a bible school that would equip and train people for ministry. If we didn't have people in the church that could go and preach and start churches we would train and raise the ministers ourselves. The Apostolic School of Ministry was birthed. It was a two-year course that trained people, in theology and how to minister under the anointing of the Holy Spirit. We wanted people to discover their gifts, recognize their calling and learn how to bring in the Kingdom of God.

For our first year, we had thirty-five students. By the starts of the second year, there were seventy students. It was exciting to see people using their gifts and discovering their place and expression in the church. During those first years, we identified the person who would pastor the new church we were starting in London. We trained many others who took their place in leadership positions within the local church in Bristol. It was an exciting time of ministry as we continued to expand and build a small network of churches.

With the church growing so fast, there were many demands and other dreams to fulfill. Since I couldn't do it on my own, it was time to employ more people. Laura was the first employee. She had been managing the administrative needs for the church while working another job but this had become increasingly difficult. Believing in teamwork, we soon employed a staff of seven people all serving in the areas of ministry they felt called to and together we saw the church grow.

Call to Nigeria

As the churches grew, a door opened to minister in Nigeria. The only problem was that they weren't letting preachers in at that time due to the country being under a dictatorship. Despite the dangers, I knew this was an opportunity of God so I moved forward and was granted a visa. I fell in love with the hot, dry environment. The people quickly became my people as I worked with Faith Victory Church, in Warri, Delta State. In the midst of tribulation and great opposition, the church in Nigeria was in a state of revival. The land was ripe with people who were hungry for the Word and moving of the Holy Spirit. I did not realize at the time that this unexpected trip would become a regular place of ministry.

The pastor of the church, Rev. Cletus Diolu had a similar heart to mine. We wanted to see people equipped and new churches started. We decided to start The Apostolic School of Ministry in Nigeria and to make this dream a reality. Within a short period of time pastors were being trained and released into new areas to grow new churches. Nigeria had stolen a place in my heart. I made regular trips for evangelistic campaigns, ministered in the churches, worked with pastors to lay strategic foundations for greater growth. The Holy Spirit moved and many healings took place in Jesus Name.

Everywhere we turned, there were ministry opportunities, whether it came through the churches we had started or other ministries that were looking for help and support. In all the years of ministry we never called a pastor and asked if we could preach for them. There was no need as we had more to do than time allowed. I was constantly on the road, between my own church and the other churches we had started or ministering in another nation. There was a great team in our local church. As other preachers took on the responsibilities of ministry, I was released to work more with other areas of church planting and networking

When I was away on ministry, Laura took hold of the mantle and with the team we had created, led the church in Bristol. We were both very busy and active in church life. Everyone that watched Laura and me saw a perfect team and ministry couple. They saw the hard work and time we spent to make the church function. This was one reason people struggled to see what went wrong in the marriage and how it all fell apart. You may have found yourself in ministry with everything going well and because of those blessings, you failed to see the devastation that's was to come. How could all this go so wrong?

Chapter 2
THE AMERICAN DREAM?

Everyone has heard of the American Dream. The term was first used by James Truslow Adams in his book *The Epic of America* which was written in 1931. He states: "The American Dream is *"that dream of a land in which life should be better and richer and fuller for everyone, with opportunity for each according to ability or achievement. It is a difficult dream for the European upper classes to interpret adequately, and too many of us ourselves have grown weary and mistrustful of it. It is not a dream of motor cars and high wages merely, but a dream of social order in which each man and each woman shall be able to attain to the fullest stature of which they are innately capable, and be recognized by others for what they are, regardless of the fortuitous circumstances of birth or position."*

Who wouldn't want the American Dream? I ministered for a number of years in the United States working with a variety of churches and pastors. The area I most frequently worked in was the beautiful "Vacation State" of Maine, in New England. During one of my trips, I was invited to minister in one of the larger, independent churches in Bangor. The church had a reputation for being on the cutting edge of ministry and because of its openness to a contemporary style of worship and moving of the Holy Spirit, it had experienced great growth. When I walked into the church that night I heard the Holy Spirit speak to my heart that I would be transplanted there and in time I would take on the leadership of the church. This surprised me. I was happy doing what I was doing and I was not ready to move. Little did I know what would take place in the coming years.

That night was an awesome time of ministry. The Word touched people's lives in a dynamic way and many were ministered to by the Holy Spirit. Even though the service went well, I was surprised that I was only invited once more to minister. Two years passed when I heard that this church had gone through leadership changes. The founding minister and Senior Pastor at that time had left the church. The church was going through a traumatic time and the people were wondering what would happen? This was when I was invited to minister again. I enter the building and I heard the Holy Spirit say again that I would be transplanted and that He had called me to lead the church. The meeting went well but I was consumed with what God had put in my heart about being transplanted. As in all things, if it's God, He didn't need me to interfere or try and make something happen.

When I returned to the UK, I spoke to Laura and told her what God had said. If this was of God, she had to know for herself that God was leading us. When I spoke to my assistant pastor, he was encouraging and open to whatever God wanted. There was nothing else I could do, so I gave it to God. I called out in prayer and told Him, I was willing to do anything and go anywhere He wanted us to go. If this was His will, I expected a call that day from someone on the Board of Directors. Within hours, the call came, but I was out of the office. A message was left for me to call back that night but I already knew what it was about. Both Laura and I were excited and nervous about the call, as we knew this could change our lives. When I finally called, I was asked if I had considered moving to Maine to take on the leadership of the church. I didn't disclose the things God had said to me because I was determined that if this was God, it would happen regardless of my belief.

That night, Laura and I agreed to visit the church and participate in a formal interview with the rest of the Board and ministry staff. There were still many obstacles to overcome. Decisions had to be made about the church network we had founded, work visas needed to be obtained and, the most difficult thing of all, was telling our families that we were moving.

Laura and I met with the Board and it was agreed that we could lead the church in the same way we had led the churches in

England with a teamwork mindset and a fivefold ministry foundation. I was promised the ability to travel for three months a year to the UK to continue my apostolic oversight of the network that had been created. All seemed good, the churches in the UK were happy and new people were released into ministry to help the local church in Bristol move forward. This was our American Dream! This new journey meant that Laura could work less and do some of the things she had hoped to do for a long time.

In the months before we left the UK, God spoke to us in many ways but the one word that stuck with me was that "this was going to be a wilderness time" I thought I understood what God was saying. We were going to Maine, "New" England which was not that much different from "old" England. It was more spiritually dry, traditional and legalistic than the rest of the United States. The church we were going to was in decline and looking to rebuild its reputation and ministry. This was going to be difficult. I thought the rebuilding of the church was going to be the challenge, but it was not the wilderness God was speaking to me about.

I have tried to show in the first part of this book, the way God spoke to me. This prompts a question of how could you hear God so much and still mess up so bad? I have endeavored to show areas of "success" as we only really understand failure when it's seen next to success. However the same is true of restoration. We only get a full understanding of Kingdom restoration when it's seen next to past success.

Broken Dreams!

The first year in Maine was great. It was the American dream! We arrived in June 2005. We had missed the long winter, arriving as everyone was enjoying the beginning of summer. We settled in and enjoyed the beauty of Maine. We had a number of family and friends who came to visit, which helped our transition of moving from one country to another. The church was open and willing to move forward. We started laying new foundations for vision and growth. The Church started to transform into a team minded ministry despite its recent decline and became exited about the future of the ministry. We shared in their joy. We felt that this was the new beginning we had hoped for. The transition from one church and country to another went well. We had the full support of family and friends and our future was before us.

After the first year, the church continued to move forward, but our marriage started to suffer. There was a great deal of strain from various directions, some church related and others were personal. Laura had been diagnosed a few years before with a life threatening disease. As long as she stayed on the right medication her symptoms were manageable. One difficulty we faced when we moved to Maine was that Laura had to use different medication that caused different side effects, mood swings and depression.

For a long time we didn't realize why she was feeling the way she was and we didn't understand how they were affecting her body. Many people gave their opinion and thought it was just the strain of moving to a new country. I wish I could say that I fully supported her through this time but I probably didn't. I did what I thought was best at that time, but I also had a church to oversee and help it through its challenges. I did what I knew which was to bury myself in work and ministry. As the months rolled on, Laura became more depressed, and often found it overwhelming to even go to the church and interact with people. The church struggled with this. They had an expectation of a ministry couple working together and they were not seeing Laura as much as they would have liked. They didn't understand the personal struggle she was going through. Despite their good intentions, their "encouragement" and "solutions" to the problem caused more stress.

As the eternal optimist, I expected things to change. The church was moving forward in some areas, but there were challenges and unspoken demands on us as a ministry couple. Laura's condition didn't improve for many months and I was pulled between two priorities. In hindsight, I took man's approach rather than a Kingdom perspective. I should have given Laura more time but I kept pushing myself to help the church.

Often when we are under pressure and things, like our marriage start to fail, it becomes easier to find an area where we are successful and concentrate on that. We are caught in the trap of doing the man thing and forgetting the God thing.

Earlier I asked the question, "How could God speak so clearly to me and yet in times like this I didn't hear His voice telling me to change my actions or my marriage would fail." Often God speaks with the still small voice, that is a thought, image, or revelation that we know is true. We can choose to listen or ignore it. It's easy to grab hold of the still small voice when it's encouraging or speaking promises for the future. We want to hear those things and run with them. When that voice warns or rebukes, requiring a change of attitude and action, we can ignore it or dismiss it as personal thoughts. No one likes to be told they are wrong or that they need to change. We make excuses for our actions and refuse to see wisdom even when others speak it. God never stops speaking we stop listening!

I am sure if you have gone through this kind of experience, you have found yourself in somewhat of a parallel world. On one hand you hear God clearly for the church and ministry but on the other hand you ignore the things God is speaking to you concerning your family. As time went by, Laura continued to struggle with her health. I found myself becoming more and more distant. I was finding love and support in different areas. I enjoyed the church family and the social interactions. I excused Laura's absences on her health, which was partially true. The warning signs were there for others to see. I ignored them.

Another stressor at that time was that we had decided to build our own house. It was another one of my "great ideas"! Why buy something that other people have lived in, when we can build something that we have designed to suit our needs. I love projects but it added pressure creating a greater demand on my time. I used this project to concentrate on to conceal or hide the issue I should have been dealing with.

Laura finally managed to work with the doctor to get her medication right. She was doing well physically, but the previous month's challenges had left scars. We realized that we had grown apart. We had many questions about church life, ministry and our marriage. Neither of us was happy. For the first time in our relationship, our conversation changed. We were no longer talking about the future but we were questioning if we should stay together. In our 20-year relationship we had never spoken of separation or used the word divorce, knowing the power of words and the damage they can do.

Just before Christmas, we had one of those conversations. We realized that our relationship had changed. What had started out good had become more of a business relationship than a marriage. We didn't argue, fight or scream at each other. We had a good friendship and to the outside world we had everything in order. We were very good at what we did and complemented each other in ministry but the spark was gone and we knew it. This was not an excuse to separate, just our reality. It was as if we both asked the question at the same time, "Should we separate? Should we divorce?" I remember the moment very clearly. As the words were spoken, something hit me. It was as if everything went dark. Something had died and in that moment the walls came up and I switched off.

The scripture is clear about the power of words and how we use them. Our words have *"the power of life and death"* and we have a choice what we speak into another's life. This doesn't mean that we should be ignorant about where we are in our relationships but we should choose our words carefully. This was a turning point in our marriage and a significant point in our separation. Laura was still struggling with the demands of the church and she was confused about what she wanted. She wasn't sure about the church, her interest in ministry or if she wanted to stay married to me. It was time for Laura to take a break. She needed space, time to think and a place she could hear God speak. We arranged for her to go to the UK and visit friends and family. This would give her time to get away and find some answers.

When Laura returned to Maine, two weeks later, she was met by church gossip and assumptions. The trip had done her good, she felt refreshed. She had discovered she still loved me and wanted to fight for our marriage to work. I was in a different place. During our time apart I had developed more questions and confusion about what I wanted. Just take a second to think about that. I was unsure of what "I" wanted. There was someone sitting on the throne of my heart and it was not God. I had slipped into the world of the carnal man and I was taking control when I should have been listening to God. The more we take control and listen to our carnal man the further we turn away from truth and make decisions that are of this world and not of the Kingdom.

I had questions about the church and ministry. The ministry and call of God had consumed my life for the past 20 years and was still my passion. I knew my heart was not right about my marriage, so to continue as pastor did not support an example of integrity. We decided it was time to talk to the church. We needed to explain where we were with our marriage and try to develop a plan of how and when we could transition leadership to others in the church. It was a difficult time for us. We had given up many things in England for the "American Dream." That dream was broken and we had to lay it down.

It was a difficult situation for the church also as they had already lost their founding pastor. Now they were faced with losing the pastor and wife they had hoped would bring change and growth.

In situations like this, there are many opinions of how to move forward but those will not be discussed here. This book is not about whether the church's decisions were right or wrong, but about the things that happened in my life that caused me to fail as a man of God.

Not only did we have to let go of the ministry in the United States, we had to let go of the ministry we were still involved in though the network of churches in England. I took the most difficult trip of my life when I returned to the UK for a week to talk to family members, friends and pastors in the various churches we were overseeing. I had to tell them that our marriage was in trouble and that we had decided to step down from ministry. It was during that trip I also resigned from overseeing the network of churches. I came back devastated. People had listened, asked questions and offered support but for the first time in my life, I was failing. It was all going wrong and with that was my greatest passion, doing the work of the ministry, which I had to let go off for a season. How had I let this happen? I was empty. All I had worked for was gone. I could still see the fruits of my labor but this was a hard and painful step.

In all the years of ministry, I had never lost a battle or failed to overcome a challenge that was before me. Like King David, I didn't care how big or imposing the giant was, God was bigger and had an answer. My attitude was that I would be victorious. But this giant was of my own making, a battle I had created and one I had lost the will to fight in! When I returned to Maine, there was more gossip and heartache. In the few weeks since we had spoken to the church, the Board of Directors decided to hand over the church to the new leaders. Our visa's only allowed us to work in for a specific ministry, the church we had just handed over. We found ourselves unable to work for another business or church and we were still building our "dream house."

With increased pressure, time was against us. Laura's health problems increased. Our relationship was at an all time low. We felt the church had abandoned us and the purpose we had in ministry together was no longer there. We decided it was time for Laura to return to the UK to be with friends and family, who could offer her the love and support she needed. I would remain in the States and finish building the house. Once the house was finished, it would be sold and we would assess what our next step would be. The drive from Bangor, Maine to Boston's Logan International Airport was difficult. We didn't know what the future would hold or where we would be. Laura was more positive, still having hope that we could make our marriage work. I was not so sure, or maybe perhaps I was less willing to fight. All that I had lived, worked and ministered for was gone. I felt broken!

At this point everyone was looking for a happy ending, like in an episode of the hit TV show "Friends" where reconciliation takes place just before the plane took off. In a Hollywood story, I would buy a ticket leaving everything behind and go with her. Unfortunately, this is not a Hollywood story but a true story of success, failure and restoration. The scene at Boston airport still hounds me and the pain is still very real. Seeing Laura arrive at check-in to make her way through customs with all her possessions in two suitcases, looking back with eyes that said, "Is this it"? Is it over?" is still painful. My gaze was as empty as hers. I returned to my car and broke down in tears. I knew it was over and that there was no way back.

Chapter 3
CRACKS IN OUR FOUNDATION

No one plans for his or her marriage to end in divorce. It is a horrible experience that destroys the soul. I would not wish on my worst enemies. I have not come through this experience waving a flag of victory, endorsing the act of getting divorced. In fact, I am more determined to help people find their way through a marital mess to find solutions and regain happiness. When you make your wedding vows to each other, you honestly believe they are forever. You look each other in the eyes and announce your intentions, believing that you will have the strength to carry through your promise of "for better or worse."

If you gone through a divorce, you can look back at your marriage with bitterness and blame everyone else for its failure or you can look in a mirror and ask yourself, "What did I do wrong?" Blaming others never brings true repentance, because you don't acknowledge that you have done anything wrong. By admitting your mistakes and truly repenting, you open the door for God to start the restoration process. Restoration is impossible without repentance.

In the book of Joel, God promises Israel restoration (*Joel 2:25*), "*restoring the years the locust have eaten*". I have heard this prayed over people, prophesied over a congregation and promised individuals. I love and get excited at this proclamation of scripture. I stand by those words and say "Amen, amen and amen." However then there is the man part, which we have to do in releasing the God part. We see man's responsibility in Joel 2:12-14 in that before the promise is released, the prophet calls the people to repent. Repentance opens the door to restoration!

The other reality is that the devil hates good marriages. Godly marriages have power! They reflect the unity of Christ and his church (*Ephesians 5:32*) they serve as an example of Christ's unconditional love and willingness to sacrifice. I believe the devil tries to sow seeds of destruction from the day you get married in an effort to destroy your unity. If we fail to take heed of the Holy Spirit showing us areas in which we need to change, we become blind and those seeds create a harvest. As Christians we are quick to see the battle we face for the hearts of men and women but we often miss the battle at home for our marriages. Often we fail to take notice of cracks in the foundation. If you were to look at your basement or foundation slab and saw a few small cracks you would probably ignore them. They can remain in the same state for years until there is a significant rainstorm or freeze and the ground moves. Once the ground moves the foundation is under intense pressure and if there is a significant crack, the slab will break at that weak point. The structure becomes unstable and the building will evenly fall if not repaired.

When I look back, it's easy to see some of the cracks in the foundation of my marriage. Many of the same problems are a challenge to anyone who is in ministry and yet if they go undetected or dealt with they will have devastating effects.

Church Foundation

Whenever there are problems you have to look back at your early years in life to see what effect the family unit had on your belief system and the way you do things. This is also true of the Christian life. Your first few years as a Christian lay a foundation for your walk and ministry. The church you first attend helps shape you as a believer. This doesn't mean that you fail to see faults or change your belief over time, but there will be some things that go undetected that need to be adjusted as you continue in your Christian walk. One of the areas that influenced me in my early years was the unspoken message that you had to learn to survive on your own!

This was not a message that was spoken from the pulpit but it was one that everyone in the church knew. From the pulpit we were encouraged to speak to our home group leaders or pastors when we had problems. However, the moment you spoke about an area you were struggling with, you were asked to sit down from ministry or take a time out. The unspoken message was, if you struggle with anything, don't talk about it or you will be judged and time will be served!

As I explained earlier, Laura and I were very young when we got married and we were passionate about the ministry and what God had called us to. When I look back at those early years, there were things in my marriage that I struggled with and would have loved to talk out with someone. The problem was, if I had spoken to anyone, I would have been given my "time out". My response was to keep my struggles to myself and to try dealing with them on my own. I didn't want to undermine my chances of fulfilling the ministry call in the local church or damage my availability for the future. It is normal as a young Christian to focus on the influence that men have rather than understand that God is in control and He is the one who opens and closes doors.

The Bible encourages us to confess our sins to one another. Why? There is power and release in confession. If you are struggling with something, it doesn't mean it's a sin issue but the power of confession remains the same. It enables you to recognize the problem and with the help of another Christian, deal with the issue you're struggling with.

> "Confess your trespasses to one another, and pray for one another, that you may be healed. The effective fervent prayer of a righteous man avails much" (James 5:16)

Confession not only brings recognition of the problem you are struggling with, but it starts the process of healing. If no one knows you are struggling, they can't help. The amount of times we have heard people moan that no one helps them is amazing, especially when the same people fail to tell anyone that they are struggling and in need of help. What happens if we don't confess and talk to someone? The problem gets bigger as you take it into isolation even though it may go under the surface and be undetected. No one knows about the struggles you are having, except you, God and the devil. God wants you to confess, not to judge you but to help you. The devil wants you to stay quiet because in a place of isolation he can manipulate and torment you. The problem becomes bigger! There is no relief from your torment even though God wants to start the mending and healing process. You haven't opened the door of your heart to allow that to take place!

I can't blame the church for keeping my struggles to myself because the Bible is clear in what I should have done. The fault is mine, not theirs. However, the belief system that was created by the church I attended is the same belief system that exists in many churches around the world and unless this problem is dealt with, many people will continue to struggle and there will continue to be casualties. I think ministers struggle more than the congregation with secret struggles. I have ministered to many people over the years, with grace and affection and yet I have feared being as open with my struggles because I thought I should know better and not have as much difficulty as the congregation. We are all flesh and blood regardless of the ministry call and therefore we have to find a way to manage our challenges.

My fear of failure and what man would say or how man would judge me resulted in my hiding some of the things I was struggling with in my marriage. This caused a crack in my foundation. When my world changed and the storms beat against the foundation the crack grew and it had a devastating effect. The problem wasn't with the challenges, it was my fear of talking about them and asking for help. I put my fear above my responsibility to my marriage. Many of us do this, but when things go undetected or are brushed aside they have a way of causing us to fall!

Ministry and Marriage

There are three major elements of relationship in the Christian life, our relationship with God, church (or ministry) and family. If our priorities are right, we will see success, but if we they are out of order, it's disastrous. All three areas are important to God, but they need to be in proper balance. Looking at couples in ministry, one often sees a relationship with God is primary, ministry responsibilities are secondary and family is third. This contradicts scripture. In Timothy, the scriptures clearly state that if we desire to be in ministry, we have to manage our own family well. God is to be first and then we are called to be the priest in the home before we are called to be the pastor in the pulpit.
(1 Timothy 3)

When our relationship with God is paramount, we must be obedient to His voice. To accomplish this, we may need the gift of discernment and wise counsel. Ministers have dreams and visions that they believe are from God, requiring obedience. God may call us to do something that will require our family to make sacrifices but that does not mean they need to suffer.

An example of this is when God calls a family to move from one location to another, to fulfill His will. God needs to be first and we need to obey, but the next priority is to make this transition as smooth as possible for the family. They may need to sacrifice some relationships but they should not suffer loss of family time, family fun, love and support. In fact, more family time may be required during a transition to help the family adjust. Once the first two priorities are set the foundation has been laid for the third area, church ministry. This appears simple but it can be difficult to find right balance.

I have been in ministry for many years. I am a man of great dreams and vision. I want to do all I can for God and see the church grow. Yet, in all my efforts, there are times when I should have taken my foot "off the pedal" of ministry and given more time to my family.

I love to work and minister. I have never gotten up in the morning and thought, "Oh no, I have to go to work!" Having been brought up with a good work ethic is positive, but if it isn't balanced and in the proper priority, it can be detrimental to other areas of life. I would find myself driven to work eighty to ninety hours a week, but Laura didn't always share my enthusiasm!

Laura and I were in ministry together. We went to the office together and left together. We both enjoyed what we were doing. We rarely fought at work because we knew what we were good at and enjoyed the work of the ministry. The people we employed enjoyed coming to work. The problem was that because we filled so much of our time together at work, we didn't take quality time for ourselves. I thought Laura was happy with our lifestyle. It was only in our final months together that we really talked about this and I realized that she had not been happy. People could say she should have spoken up, but the truth is that it was my responsibility to put my family's needs before the ministry. Failing to have my priorities in proper order was another crack in our foundation.

I often wonder how life would have been different had I listened to wise counsel when "date nights" were suggested or heard the whisper of the Holy Spirit when Laura had needs. I did not understand that sacrifice did not require suffering. God has worked with me to teach me this lesson over the last few years, but unfortunately my blindness still created casualties. The Bible says, *"Whatsoever a man sows that he shall reap". (Galatians 6:7)* The law of sowing and reaping is evident in everything we do. Wherever we sow, we get a harvest. At the end of my marriage with Laura, we both recognized we were a good team in work and ministry. This is where we sowed most of our time. If we had sowed more time into our relationship, outside the ministry, our marriage would have been stronger and endured the storms of life.

I want to encourage you, as individuals and ministers, to get priorities straight in your life; God first, family needs second and then church (ministry). Strive to find the right balance between time you spend investing in your marriage and your ministry. We are living in a time where more and more marriages in the ministry end in divorce. Let's learn the lessons from the past or from people that have suffered through divorce and "stop the rot."

House Invasion

As ministers, there is a heart-felt passion to reach out to the hurt, lost and those in pain who need support. We have a great example in Jesus, who reached out to the lost sheep of Israel and ministered to the bruised and battered, carrying them on his shoulders. There are always people that need to be carried. They require time and energy, but there comes a point that we have to put them down and let them walk on their own. If we fail to let go and let the wounded learn to walk on their own again, the burden becomes more than that which Christ has required.

This brings me to the third crack in our foundation. From the time Laura and I were married, we had an "Open Home" mentality which meant anyone could come into our home and find refuge, support, encouragement and even a bed for the night. For years we reached out to many people and we witnessed miraculous results of people being healed and changed. When we started the church in Bristol, we took this to the next level. There were two individuals who not only needed help, but a home to live in as well. After prayerful consideration, we believed that God led us to give these people a home to live in. We offered support and created a family environment allowing them to flourish. In both cases the plan was to be offer a short-term solution to help them move forward in their life and Christian walk.

What started out being of God, ended up becoming a man thing as we stopped listening to God and thinking we knew a better way. One person ended up living with us for ten years! In the first few years we saw great improvements. When I look back now,

I know there came a time when we should have encouraged that individual to move out and get on with their life. Out of our own love we did the man thing and let that time go on and on. This resulted in losing the grace of God to deal with the situation and at the same time it caused our personal time to be overtaken until the burden became unbearable.

The other person who stayed with us, was a young girl called Babz. After losing both of her parents by the age of sixteen, she came to live with us for a year. The time came when we had encouraged her to move on in her life. It was hard to let her go as it seemed at the time that she was not as far along in her Christian walk as the person who stayed with us for ten years. However, at the time of this writing, Babz is moving forward in her walk with God in a very encouraging way. She received the physical love and support she needed for a time and then she was ready to move on, allowing God to provide for her and guide her in her walk.

There are many things in ministry, which God tells us to do. They require time and sacrifice, but when it's God, He gives us the grace and wisdom to deal with those areas. Like many things they are for a season and it's important that we discern when the season is over. If we continue to sow seed in the wrong season it will not produce a harvest and yet we have still given our time and energy into planting that seed.

Where are you giving your time? Is it a God thing or has it become a man thing? Perhaps it's not time given to individuals, as in my situation, but it could be organized church events, prayer meetings, community projects or a mission's effort. God may inspire all these events, but we have to be led by the Holy Spirit and realize that nothing is meant to last forever. God calls programs or activities in the church for a season. Once that season is over, if they continue, they may become a burden that takes away from your relationship with your wife, creating a crack in your foundation.

I have mentioned three areas in which there were cracks in our foundation. This is not a complete list but it encompasses the areas I have been led to write about. It's important for you to read this and examine your life asking the question, "Where are there cracks in my foundation?" You have the chance to change them. If nothing changes, the results won't change either. If you base future relationships on the same principles and actions as your last relationship, it will probably end the same way.

Chapter 4
THE WILDERNESS

Before I moved to Maine, God spoke to me and said that "It was going to be a wilderness experience" I was to learn that the wilderness I expected and the one God was talking about were very different. When Christians speak of a wilderness experience, we are talking about a season in our life when it becomes more difficult than our "normal" Christian walk. The wilderness speaks of a desert, a lonely place or a place of isolation. It's not the green pastures and fruitfulness that we desire.

There are a number of reasons why we go through wilderness experiences. The first is because, like Jesus we are *"led there by the Holy Spirit" (Luke 4:1)* for a God given purpose. When Jesus was led into the wilderness, it was a time of teaching, training and learning to overcome the devil. Jesus came out of the wilderness and *"returned in the power of the Spirit" (Luke 4:14)*. If we stay positive in the wilderness and continue to look to God for help and support, then we will learn many valuable lessons. Like Jesus, we will come out of the season with our life improved and with the fullness of the Holy Spirit.

Take a moment to ponder the progression in Jesus' life after he came through his wilderness experience. The Bible says he entered the wilderness *"filled with the Holy Spirit"* and he came out *"in the power of the Spirit."* The wilderness may seem like the hardest time in our life but is it is also the time we learn and are empowered to move forward. It is like the illustration of mountaintop Christians and those in the valley. We all want to be on the mountaintop to see the horizon and the Promised Land before us. However, nothing good grows on mountaintops, good things grow in valleys. We often grow more in the wilderness than in the Promised Land.

The second wilderness is the result of us putting ourselves there due to sin. Like Moses we try to do things our way

(Exodus 2:11-16). Moses saw an Egyptian fighting with a Hebrew man. He decided to get involved and rescue the Hebrew man, killing the Egyptian. God had put something in Moses' heart to rescue the Children of Israel, but this was neither the time nor the way God intended it to happen. Whenever we become lord of our own lives and stop listening to God, we get ourselves in trouble. We walk out of fruitfulness into the wilderness. Although we put ourselves in the wilderness due to our own choices and mistakes, God never leaves us. We can see from the life of Moses that God was with him as he taught him new things that would help with his future.

For forty years Moses had learned in the house of an Egyptian. As the adopted son of pharaoh, he learned how to lead as the world leads. After killing the Egyptian he escaped to the wilderness and became a sheep farmer. It was there that he learned how to lead as God leads. After forty years in the wilderness, God called Moses and commissioned him to deliver the Children of Israel. However, this time he would rescue them the way God intended and he would lead them out of captivity, not with a golden scepter like Pharaoh's but with a Shepherd's crook. It didn't look as glamorous as the golden scepter but when God told him to stretch it out, miracles happened. God's methods are always better than man's, and by God's grace, Moses learned this after he had sinned. God turns all things for good, even when we have made big mistakes. God takes hold of our lives while we are in the wilderness for the purpose of bringing us out better equipped to serve the kingdom of God. God never changed the call He placed on Moses but He graciously restored him. *(Acts 7:17-36)*

The third type of wilderness is the most difficult. God led the Children of Israel out of the captivity of the Egyptians into the wilderness. Their wilderness season to journey to the Promised Land was meant to be for approximately ten months. They had the best leader in Moses who knew the wilderness well. He knew how to live, walk and navigate his way through this terrain. However, their lack of faith and inability to see beyond the obstacles caused them to doubt and question God. The children of Israel remained in the wilderness for forty years. The generation that had been given the promise and the potential of a better life, in a better land, never saw it because they were forever looking back and talking negatively, not believing in their quest. They only saw the obstacles and problems. They declared themselves unfit for the promises of God *(Numbers 14)*. There are many people today in the church that have the same attitude. They never see the good things of God, just their own inabilities. They are always moaning about what others have and what they don't have. Unfortunately, their attitude keeps them in the wilderness and out of the promises that God so desperately wants them to inherit.

These negative people surrounded Joshua and Caleb but they never allowed the unbelief to restrict their own faith in God. As a result, both Joshua and Caleb came out of the wilderness and possessed the promises of God *(Numbers 14:22-24)*. We all go through wilderness seasons, whether we are led into them by the Holy Spirit or whether we find ourselves there through sin. The length of time in the wilderness depends on our willingness to learn, change and keep the faith. If all we do is moan, and complain about our situation and declare that we are without hope, we will never get through this season and we will probably stay in the wilderness a long time. God does not want us there forever, just for a season as we learn the lessons needed to have a positive influence on our tomorrow.

I experienced my wilderness when Laura returned to England. It was a wilderness that could have been avoided but it was not. In the midst of the storm of challenges I had faced over the previous year, I took my eyes off Jesus and started to make decisions for myself. Laura returned to England and I remained in Maine to finish building the house, so it could be sold. It appeared that there was no other choice as we had invested our life savings into the project. Walking away would cause us to lose everything.

In the days and weeks to come, I made decisions that not only caused our separation to be permanent, but also led to divorce. For several months before my resignation and during Laura's depression, I found myself looking for support and friendship from others. As a minister, I should have demonstrated more wisdom, but I found that support and friendship with another person who was also going through the same struggles in her marriage.

Amanda had been a Christian for many years and part of the leadership team in the church. She had a dynamic personality that was larger than life and the ability to make me laugh. In the midst of all that was happening and the pain at home, I found joy in her company. She had been struggling in her marriage for years and she understood the things I was going through. I can hear you scream," Don't be stupid! What are you doing? Isn't this the blind leading the blind?" In the clear light of day I can answer," Yes, yes, yes!" However, under the circumstances, it was easier to deny the facts. I was aching for some joy. Despite the wisdom from years in ministry, when I was the lowest place in my life, Amanda was a shoulder to lean on and someone who I could talk to.

After Laura left Maine to return to the UK, the friendship Amanda and I had, accelerated. Amanda was already separated from her husband and we were two lonely people trying to make our way through life's hurdles. In the midst of all the confusion and feelings of rejection we found joy and happiness in each other's presence. The relationship we had, developed quickly and before long our relationship deepened and we became inseparable. It was exhilarating to be with Amanda. We knew deep down it was wrong, but we went with what felt good. We both used the excuse that we were separated, but the truth remained that I was still married and this was an act of adultery. Not only had I lost everything in ministry, I was now living a life of sin.

I had gone from being full of joy, loving and serving God, successful in ministry, enjoying every moment of life, surrounded by lots of family and friends, to being out of work and ministry, isolated from my family in England, separated from my wife and the only person I had to talk to was Amanda. This is not to make excuses for the mistakes we made, but it puts the situation in a realistic context. It also highlights another truth. Often when people are in a low place, when they have experienced grief and loss, they look for something to fill the void. This does not excuse the sin, but it should encourage us to become our brother's keeper. When we see these things happen we need to offer an appropriate listening ear, or a place of comfort, support, and Godly advise.

During this time, my mind was confused from events and people wounded my heart. I was faced with a whirlwind of thoughts and emotion, yet in the midst of the confusion, I had fallen in love with Amanda and chose to pursue our relationship. As you can imagine, this was the "nail in the coffin" in my marriage to Laura. We both realized that it was the end of our twenty-year relationship. There were many tears for both of us. It's not easy to walk away from one relationship and just get on with another. You don't stop caring, worrying or wanting the best for the other person. It is hard to live with the realization of all the pain you have caused them. How do you let go of the memories of all you did together in ministry and the promises, hopes and dreams you had together? These are some of the hurdles that have to be faced and you realize why God hates divorce.

As my relationship with Laura came to an end, my relationship with Amanda and her three children grew. I know that God hates sin and divorce. This was not God's choice, just like it wasn't God's choice for Moses to kill the Egyptian man. I, like Moses, had stepped outside of the will of God and pursued my own desires. I was about to enter a wilderness period that would be very difficult, yet in the midst of it I would discover the love and grace of God like never before. The Bible is clear that God turns all things for good. He knows the mistakes we have made and are going to make. In an amazing way, God used this wilderness period to teach me valuable lessons and prepare me again for ministry. God dealt with my heart and my relationship with Amanda, through repentance and brought grace and hope into our relationship. In time, we recommitted our lives to God and to each other in marriage.

Broken

Anyone who goes through any type of loss or divorce will feel broken. Facing up to personal failure, the loss of friends, and the rejection you face will cause you to feel crushed. Another consequence is the feeling of distance in your relationship with God. This is not God pulling away from you, but you struggling to accept God's grace as you look through the window of pain.

No one chooses to go through this kind of pain. I never wanted to run from God but into His arms. During the days of my separation and divorce, there was never a point when I felt I didn't want Jesus in my life. I knew I was wrong and I wanted to repent. That's what I thought I was doing. The reality was that if I were really repenting, I would have changed my ways. What I was really doing was having a pity party. I thought I was saying "sorry" to God, but I was just saying that I hated how hard life had become.

Before true repentance, brokenness has to take place. David speaks of this in Psalm 51:

> The sacrifices of God are a broken spirit, a broken and contrite heart. These, O God, you will not despise. (Psalm 51:17)

King David wrote this Psalm after he had an affair with Bathsheba and had her husband killed. David did not truly repent initially. Repentance came only when the Prophet Nathan revealed his sin and he was faced with loosing everything (1 Samuel 12:11-13). This brought true brokenness in David. The Psalm was written out of when David realized that God required more from him than an animal sacrificed as a sin offering. David could have obeyed the law, brought the sin offering and said he was sorry, but without a true repentant heart, what value did the offering have? We can come to God and say we are sorry, but without true repentance, it means nothing.

God is looks for brokenness. When we are tired of doing things our way and we surrender, then we choose to make Jesus our Lord again, giving Him the throne of our hearts and allowing Him to reign again. It is easy to talk about repentance and restoration but it is necessary to include brokenness because that is what leads to true repentance.

My brokenness came through situations that I felt were unfair and unjustified. I do not believe God sent them but they were the consequence of my actions and man's inability to understand grace. When we fail as ministers and individuals, we face responses from other people who are also hurting. Often their pain is a reaction to our sin and their inability to cope with it. Their defense is to withdraw and either ignore what has happened or attack, making judgment about our sin. No matter how people treat you, God is looking for the right response. Remember, if all we do is moan and complain we will prolong our wilderness experience. If we see it for what it is, and learn to deal with it, we will come through the wilderness faster and enter into the Promised Land.

Have you ever wondered where everyone has gone? I went from being popular; overseeing a number of churches with many friends around the world and within a short period of time, most of them disappeared. This is one of the consequences of divorce. People don't know how to cope with your situation, especially if you are a minister or leader. You should be above this! This was the first part of my brokenness. King David speaks of a time when he was rejected by King Saul, forced out of the palace and into the wilderness. He found himself there on his own, lonely and desperate and the only person that reached out to him was Saul's son, Jonathan.

And David stayed in the stronghold of the wilderness, and remained in the mountains in the Wilderness of Ziph. Saul sought him every day, but God did not deliver him into his hand (1 Samuel 23:14)

Then Jonathan, Saul's son, arose and went to David in the woods and strengthened his hand in God (1 Samuel 23:16)

When you go through divorce, you lose friends. There are those who were friends with you and your spouse and they usually choose whom they are going to support. Many of the joint-friends we had, lived in England, so when Laura returned, she received their support. This was great for her and good of them to do, but it left me isolated.

Regarding the church and church friends, I had resigned from the church while I was still with Laura. After she left and my relationship deepened with Amanda, the friends we had in the church struggled with this new relationship. This was understandable but I still desired a Christ-like response despite my less than Christ-like actions. What a paradox! Despite my expectations, the church congregation separated themselves from me. This is not uncommon. As a minister I understood that the church needed to take a stand but it was still a struggle to understand why all our church friends seemed to back off as well. The problem was if they stayed in touch, they were scrutinized and it created conflict within the church. They were then in danger of being isolated, so it was easier for them to isolate themselves from us. Some people totally disagreed with what we were doing and didn't feel they could have fellowship with us. This is the process that brings brokenness. I am not asking here, what Jesus would do in this situation; we will leave that for a later chapter.

There were ministers with whom I had enjoyed many hours of fellowship and ministry together. They seemed to disappear over night. Again, this is because the Bible is clear about how God hates divorce; however the Bible is also clear about forgiveness and grace. When people are afraid of what others might think if they stay in fellowship with you, or they don't know how to help bring restoration, they stop calling you.

For the person experiencing the divorce it is difficult because if you hadn't agreed with divorce, you now find yourself in a situation you never expected to be in. A forbidden line has been crossed and it is unclear how to deal with this new challenge. You don't know how people will react, so you retreat in the opposite direction and find yourself isolated in a wilderness. No matter what your experience, if you have gone through separation or divorce you will feel some kind of isolation.

This was a place of great brokenness for me. The only person I really had was Amanda, who was supportive but she was going through these things herself. My family called me daily but being three thousand miles away I still longed for personal contact. Not only did I feel isolated and lonely, but also I was unable to work. My visa only allowed me to work for that particular church, so when I resigned, I couldn't get another job. I was left on my own for most of the day, with nothing but my own questions, thoughts and fears. I couldn't just go out and meet people, because I had no income and I needed every penny I had saved to survive and complete the building of my home.

One comical thing happened that didn't seem funny at the time; I lost my driver's license. I had been driving for years and I had only been caught speeding once in twenty years. When I moved to the States, I had a period of time before I needed to take my driving test to receive a Maine license. I was an experienced driver and had a clean license. Then on one particular afternoon, I was on my way to meet some friends for coffee and I was running late. So I took the risk, put my foot to the peddle, and you guessed it, I soon saw blue flashing lights. I was stopped for speeding and because this was my first year of holding a Maine license, my speeding fine caused me to lose my license for thirty days! I was isolated and trapped in the middle of the country, with nowhere to run or hide. My first response was to moan and complain at my fate. Then the realization hit me that when you step out of the will of

God, everything starts to crumble like a house of cards. I could blame other people for isolating me or I could view my actions as wrong and God would turn this to good. The real question was, had people isolated me or was God hiding me?

There is an incredible insight in the process of God hiding us for a season. In 1 Kings 16 and 17 we read of the Prophet Elijah, who seemed to burst on the scene from nowhere. One day, he received a corrective, prophetic word from God, to give to the King of Israel, Ahab. The king had disobeyed God, by worshiping false gods. When Elijah had delivered his prophetic word of correction, God gave him another instruction to hide himself. Not out of fear, but out of obedience. God had a plan.

> Then the word of The Lord came to him saying, "get away from here and turn eastward, and hide by the Brook Cherith, which flows into the Jordan". (1 Kings 17:2-3)

God brought him to a place of isolation. With no one else around, he had to trust God. He drank from the river and God brought him food everyday through ravens. God was teaching him to keep his eyes on the Provider and to trust God and not man. In out times of isolation, we quickly realize that men and women who we thought we could trust, we can't. We have to look to God as our source of comfort, help, direction, strength and supply.

However, there is an even bigger lesson here. God led him to the brook Cherith, which means "cutting." This brook led into the Jordon which is symbolic as the place of baptism and death, or the place we die to self. In the season of isolation, God starts to cut away at our flesh, revealing our sins, character flaws, wrong thinking, and unhealthy motives. It is in this place that we have to learn to look in a mirror, see our own faults, and stop blaming everyone else for our situation. As God starts to cut (Cherith) away at our flesh and carnal desires, it leads to death (Jordon), and we are brought to a place where we die to self and start living for God again. Jesus spoke to his disciples *(Luke 14:26)* and encouraged them to crucify the flesh by bearing their own cross.

True repentance cannot come if we are not aware of our sins. We can look at circumstances we have gone through such as a divorce, but what led us to that place? If all we do is repent of the action of getting a divorce, we have left the root problems in place which can create the same situation again in the future. God knows that we will make mistakes and He desires that we learn from them. He does not want us to make the same mistake time and again. If you have divorced more than once, you have to ask the question, "Is this just an unfortunate situation or have I repeated the same behaviors and made the same poor choices that led to my first divorce?"

When we are in a place of hiding, we can choose to wallow in the situation or start to call upon Jesus, reigniting our relationship with Him. What most of us do is start off wallowing in self-pity, and then we have an occasional day of calling on Jesus. Slowly we realize that calling on Jesus leaves us happier and we start to leave the wallowing behind and push forward in our relationship with Him.

The process of being cut open to have disease removed from the body is a painful process. It's not easy. It's not a vacation. There will be days when all we seem to do is cry and say we are sorry for everything. We will remember conversations and times when we could have made different choices that would have produced different outcomes and again we are brought to our knees in tears. There will be moments when we stop thinking of our own pain and think of the pain that others have gone through because of our choices. This pain will cause us to cry out to God again and again. All of this is a part of the brokenness that leads to true repentance.

After Elijah was directed by God to leave the brook Cherith, He commanded him to go to a place called Zarephath, which means "furnace of refining" *(1 Kings 17:9.)* This was to prepare Elijah to continue his ministry of miracles and directing the King and children of Israel. God desires to remove the flesh and burn up the imperfection, so he can produce people of character and vessels of honor. God is not finished with us. He will prepare us to run and fight again. We may have lost a battle but we have not lost the war! God wants to heal His bruised and wounded. However, as the great physician He has to diagnose the problem before He can treat the problem. As soon as I realized that it was God hiding me and dealing with my heart, the quicker the healing process started to take place.

I can honestly say that there were days that I hated the loneliness and isolation. I would wonder if this would ever end or if I would ever have friends again. I didn't always understand how God could let this happen and why He wasn't presenting more godly people to rescue me. As I have come through this, looking back, I understand the importance of isolation. No man could have said the things God said to me and gotten away with it. No individual could have comforted me or spoken grace in my times of self-hatred, and brought peace in the midst of pain and tears. When people rejected me, God received me. When others spoke against me and wrote me off as the pastor who "used to be", God called me His son and continued to impart dreams for the future. When people wouldn't stop speaking of my failure and sin, God continued to tell me of His love and forgiveness.

We die In the place of Isolation. You may ask, "How long will this season last?" The answer is easy; it lasts until we are dead. When do we know we are dead? Dead men or women don't moan, complain, point the finger, look for revenge or retaliate to lies and offences pointed at them. Dead people don't react! There is no place for the flesh when the Spirit is alive and in control. It is then that the fruit of the Spirit is exhibited in our daily lives and people can see the difference. The season of isolation and the time of dealing with the flesh, dying to self, produces a more equipped person who will have a greater impact on the Kingdom of God in the future. Jesus put it this way:

"Most assuredly, I say to you, unless a grain of wheat falls into the ground and dies, it remains alone; but if it dies, it produces much grain." (John 12:24)

The wilderness of Shur (Bitterness)

No matter what mistakes we have made, sins we have committed or pain we have inflicted on others by our choices and actions, we have this human frailty to focus on what others have done to us and get mad about it. No matter how righteous or unrighteous we have been in our journey of life, no matter the circumstances surrounding the situation, we at some point, come face to face with the ugly disease of bitterness. Yes, it is a disease! Many people describe bitterness this way because it has the ability to eat away at us, increasing its destructiveness. It will undermine our personality, joy and everything that is good about us. It's like a cancer, that spreads and it needs to be dealt with. We cannot allow any amount of it to remain within us because it will return with vengeance. It's a disease that needs to be faced, operated on and completely removed.

Everyone who goes through a wilderness experience will have to fight this giant at some point. Exodus 12 tells us of Israel's miraculous journey out of Egypt. They were led by the Holy Spirit, through the Red Sea and after eighteen days they found themselves in the wilderness of Shur *(Exodus 15:22)* which is translated "Wall". Yes, they came to a wall in their journey. They were desperately in need of water but the Bible tells us that the water was "bitter". Imagine their pain, fear, anger, displeasure and grief. They had come out of Egypt with a promise of a better land and the great leader, Moses led them to a place where the water was bitter. The people did what most of us do when we find ourselves in a wilderness or unwanted situation. They complained and moaned. Imagine them shaking their fists at Moses and asking, "Why have you done this to us?" They wanted revenge, they wanted someone to blame, because it's unfair!

One of the first things we learn about bitterness is that it comes out of disappointment. The children of Israel were disappointed. They had been promised much and at this moment in time it didn't seem like they were going to see the promises of God. If we take a moment to think of the things that have caused us to be bitter, we will realize that at the root of it, is disappointment. Whether it's a place we have arrived at in our life that was unexpected or because people have disappointed us and let us down, we have a choice to hold onto the disappointment or move beyond it. It is humbling to remember that for every person that has disappointed us, we have disappointed someone else.

The waters remained bitter until the Lord instructed Moses to throw a tree (which is symbolic of the cross) into the water and it was made sweet and the people were able to drink the water. (Exodus 15:25). We are no different than the children of Israel. We become bitter at life's situations and hardships and even when we think we have seen the worst of it, the journey can seem to get harder. We wonder where God is, what is He doing and how He could allow this to happen to us. This attitude eats away at us and not only effects our emotions, but can consume our heart and spiritual being. It also impacts the people around us. The only true way to deal with bitterness is to bring it to the cross. By throwing the tree (or the cross) into the problem, we realize that we are not so great and that as Jesus has forgiven us for what we have done, so we must forgive others. If we fail to do so, we will remain in the wilderness of Shur, or the place of the wall.

Bitterness was another ugly thing I had to face in my situation. I couldn't have felt any lower or more grieved than I was. I was failing, going through a divorce, resigning from the ministry, building a house to sell and wondering what would my future hold. My life became full of disappointments. Just when I thought I was through it all, those people that I thought were my friends started speaking against me. The so-called "gracious church" became judgmental and condemning. Individuals would no longer stay in the same room as Amanda and me, because they were afraid that our sin would affect them. Close friends, whom I had stood by for many years in difficult situations, stopped calling. Individuals I thought were close to me, suddenly started speaking outrageous lies, as they struggled with their own feelings. They couldn't cope with where I was at, so they lashed out by making up stories.

Lies, gossip and judgmental words do not stop overnight. They continued to follow me for some time, and created within me feelings of bitterness and anger. What was I going to do with them?

Bitterness and anger have to be dealt with, or they will destroy us. The natural response is to retaliate but the Kingdom response is to pray for our enemies. An English prophet by the name of Graham Cook describes people who challenge us with these situations as "grace growers". They grow grace in us. They give us opportunities to develop the heart of God and the fruit of the Spirit. Everything within us, wants to avenge the wrongs that have be directed at us, but God desires that we look at how our wrongs have caused pain to others.

Brokenness is not about pointing the finger but looking in the mirror. If we retaliate we become puppets in the Devil's hands and we become a vehicle to destroy our brother. When we repay good for evil, kindness for meanness, and love for hate, we allow grace to grow in us and in those who wrong us.

If we don't address the bitterness, we will live the rest of our lives miserable. The people who have wronged us get on with their lives and we are still stuck in the pain. We continue moaning, complaining, gossiping and talking about what we used to do, instead of moving into what God has for us now!

Another man dies in the bitterness of his soul. Never having eaten with pleasure. (Job 21:25)

And do not grieve the Holy Spirit of God, by whom you were sealed for the day of redemption, Let all bitterness, wrath, anger, clamor and evil speaking be put away from you, with all malice. And be kind to one another, tenderhearted, forgiving one another even as Christ has forgiven you. (Ephesians 4:30-32)

Bitterness is a hard thing to overcome but it must be dealt with to move on and into the promises of God. We can see from the scripture above that bitterness grieves the Holy Spirit. When we are in the wilderness the last thing we want to do is push the Holy Spirit away by grieving Him. He is the one who will lead us through the wilderness and empower us to do the greater works of the kingdom *(Luke 4:1,14)*. We need to repent and become more Christ like, even when others around us are not.

It's in these times that we have to trust God to vindicate us. Most people think vindication is God punishing the people who have wronged us. That is the worldly perspective of revenge. When the people who hurt and wrong us are fellow Christians, the sting is greatest. For God to judge or punish them in the way we think He should, would just cause more pain. Do we think of them and ask ourselves, "Have they gotten their just rewards yet?" Doesn't this come from our own bitter attitude and our desperately wanting God to judge them for their wrongs? If this mindset is true, then shouldn't God also judge us for our wrongs? God tells us to pray for our enemies, not to curse them. In fact, when we read how Jesus tells us to pray regarding our sins and the sins others have committed against us we are told to ask for forgiveness on our behalf and theirs. This is radical Kingdom thinking:

"And forgive us our debts, as we forgive our debtors." (Matthew 6:12)

The way God vindicates you is that He convicts the heart of those who have sinned against you. If individuals lie about you, God in His time will reveal the truth. Those who have judged you will see God's grace on you. Throughout my journey of restoration, God has continued to reveal the truth. He has allowed others to see my heart and His blessings continue to be increased in my life making His favor undeniable. God's vindication is His hand on my life. Don't look for revenge; look for God's blessing.

When we read of Israel's experience in the wilderness of Shur and the bitterness they faced, we are encouraged to see that they overcame and the bitter waters became sweet. *(Exodus 15:25).* We can almost hear the sigh of relief and feel the joy that came with their release. They could drink again and move on in hope. The scripture goes on to say of God, *"That I am the Lord who heals you." (Exodus 15:26)* The only true way of overcoming is through our trust, prayer, meditation and help from Jesus. He is our healer and the more we understand the grace He has towards us, we will be gracious towards others. The more we see His love in a hostile environment, the more we will be able to love others but the greatest miracle is His ability to forgive us our wrongs and sins. The Bible tells us, *"freely we have received, freely we must give". (Matthew 10:8)* I have preached and encouraged people from this scripture many times to show others the grace that God has shown them. This is easy to do and to extend grace to others when we are in a good place. It becomes harder when we need to rely on the strength and direction of the Holy Spirit while we are in the wilderness.

Moving away from bitterness is a choice. It can be a daily battle. We may choose to forgive and then something happens that triggers a memory and we are back complaining about that old situation. Stop complaining. Let it go or the bitterness of that painful situation will come back. The children of Israel moved on from Shur. It stopped being a wall for them and they were able to come to a place called Elim *(Exodus 15:27).* It was here where they discovered twelve springs of water and seventy palm trees. When we deal with our bitterness, God will bring us to a place of shelter. When we let God in, the Holy Spirit will refresh our hearts and strengthen us to continue this journey to a place of new life and into the Promised Land.

Chapter 5
LEPERS IN THE CHURCH

As ministers of God we can try to run, but we can't hide. The call of God has been written on our heart with an unmovable marker. It's imprinted; God has shaped, molded and created a dream that cannot be shaken. We can be like Jonah and run and all that happens is that we end up in the belly of a fish or some other place that stinks. So we can take hold of the call of God and work towards it being obedient to the promises of God or we can try and run from it, never succeeding and unable to find contentment.

This is a difficult thing to face when we know we are in a place we shouldn't be. The fact remains that God is unrepentant. He continues to call and He will not let us go. We can't shake it, run from it or disguise it. It is who we are. We are called and appointed by God. He did not make a mistake. We make mistakes but He knew we were going to make them even before we crossed the line. He is an all-knowing God. Even knowing what we were going to do, He still called us. *(Romans 11:29)*

For me, His call was a thought that was always in my mind and heart. I knew that I had resigned from my ministry position and that I had made some ungodly choices, but my heart's desire remained the same. I would wake up in the morning in tears. When I left Amanda at night and went home again, I would be in tears, crying out to God for help. I wanted Him to lead me. I wanted the things He had called me to. I would dream about preaching, ministering, and helping people. God was chasing after me and He would not let me go. I had to start to put things right. I couldn't run any longer.

I had not been to church for a number of months. I really didn't know where to go and was afraid to go anywhere because of what people might say or think of me. I was living in a small city and I had been the minister of one of the most well known churches in the area. My face had been on TV and in the newspapers a number of times and to make matters worse, I had a British accent. How many preachers had a British accent in Bangor Maine? I would be quickly identified and the decisions I had made would quickly be present in the thoughts of the other church members. Knowing what the church can be like, I knew they would not hold back their opinions. I felt that our future would be in their hands. I made the excuse to myself that I didn't want to cause any minister grief. I didn't want them to face hard decisions or conversations because I went to "their" church. The truth was I was afraid of what I might face. Yet I knew that if I wanted to get my life back on track and if I ever wanted to fulfill the ministry call in the future, I had to get back into the church.

I also knew it was the heart of God. The church is meant to be the place of healing, exhortation, help, support, a place where we can be forgiven, restored and brought back into the place that God wants us.

> *Not forsaking the assembling of ourselves together, as is the manner of some, but exhorting one another and so much the more as you see the Day approaching. (Hebrews 10:25)*

There are many hurting people who have made mistakes or feel like they are not wanted in a particular church, and so they stay away. We have to get past this and move back to church. Now I can hear some of you say, "You don't know what I faced and what the church was like!" Well my initial experience showed me what I had hoped the church wasn't! As a minister, I came to understand that people make mistakes. It is the responsibility of the church, and the people in it, to show the heart and character of Christ by extending grace. This does not mean we agree with a person's sin, but that we work with the individual to bring them to a place of repentance and restoration. Since this was my philosophy, it was also my expectation.

After a number of discussions, and much fear, Amanda and I decided to bring her three children with us to go to a local church. We thought it was large enough, with over six hundred people for us to hide. We both wanted a place where we could worship and allow the Spirit of God to speak to us and begin putting the wrongs in our life right. Our first Sunday went well. In the midst of good praise and worship and many tears of conviction, we listened to the Word, enjoyed the service and left wanting more. There were a number of people that knew us, and on the surface they seemed nice and welcomed us. We left making a decision that we would continue to come to this church.

The second service also went well; we even responded to an altar call and received Holy Spirit ministry. Again, it seemed we were being welcomed but then we started to notice that other people were becoming aware of our presence. We knew that rumors, lies and some truth were going around the churches about us and we watched as people responded. We were willing to talk and share with anyone that wanted answers from us. As the weeks went by, we noticed a particular elder continually staring at us with disgust. Initially, I thought I was just being paranoid, but it soon became obvious that was not the case. There were others who would reach out their hand and welcome us, but you could see them pointing and talking about us as we walked away.

We started to feel more and more uncomfortable. I imagined myself like a person in the New Testament that had leprosy. No one wanted to go near them, or talk with them, afraid that they might catch the disease from the leper. We started to feel isolated but decided we needed to persevere as God wanted us in church and this was as good as any.

The time came for me to organize a meeting with the minister. We had been going to the church for a number of weeks. He knew who I was and I felt obligated to talk to him about our situation, so I invited him for coffee!

I thought it was a good meeting. The minister listened to all I had to say as I told him everything about my broken relationship with Laura, all that had happened in the previous church, my present situation and my relationship with Amanda. I included the areas where I saw we still needed to change. I expressed that we were looking for a place to worship and receive strength and encouragement. We wanted to deal with our sin, but we needed some support. Some people may be of the opinion that we should have dealt with all our sin before we tried going back to church. In the mist of our situation we knew there were things wrong, and we could list the things that we considered more sinful than others. However, the truth remains that we were struggling with a number of issues and wanted a church that would stand by us, and help us get back to the place that Christ wanted us to be.

After a couple of hours, the minister had been moved to tears, unable to comprehend the things we had been through and the pain we had endured. With great passion he prayed for me, asking God to give me hope, to bring forgiveness, and for the promise of restoration and grace. All seemed well, but then as he was about to leave, he informed me that we were no longer welcome in the church as a couple. Either one of us could attend, but we could not go together. The elders in the church had been talking and had made the decision. My paranoia had had some truth to it! You can imagine my pain. After all we had been through, I had hoped the church would not accept or excuse our sin, but that it would be willing to help us on the road of recovery.

I have heard it said and preached it myself many times, that in regards to winning the unsaved, you cast the net wide and draw in the dirty smelly fish (symbolic of unbelievers). We have not been commanded by God to wash the fish before we catch them! When an unbeliever comes to a church, they are dirty, smelly and full of sin. Once they have made a commitment to Christ, the Holy Spirit starts to work on their character, convicting them of sin and the things they need to change. The ministers and leaders in the church are there to help support the new believer in their new life in Christ Jesus. The process is no different for a fallen minister or any individual that has made mistakes. We have to get back to a place where we allow the Holy Spirit to move and bring change in our lives. With the minister's help, we are brought to a place of repentance, healing and restoration.

Unfortunately many churches struggle with sin and restoration. Those who have fallen are made to feel like a leper, who is not allowed in the presence of "holy" Christians. The fear is that if the minister accepted us that this may cause church members to stray. If the minister accepted a fallen minister, it could be assumed that it is acceptable to do whatever sin you want, and simply be accepted and restored. It would appear they were giving a license to sin. Jesus was able to strike a balance in grace and truth, in forgiveness and correction. Jesus always reached out to the sinner. He was often found sitting in the presence of sinners, sharing a meal. Jesus met people at their level. He was able to reach out to the sinner while not letting their sin or past conduct affect his righteousness or walk. He modeled both truth and grace. He hated the sin, but loved the sinner. He didn't come for the righteous but the unrighteous and so with love He reached out with grace. (Matthew 9:13)

Due to the response we received, Amanda and I felt like lepers in the church. We felt rejected and marginalized. There were times we wanted to leave Bangor, and move to a place where no one knew us. But we knew that we were in the right place at this time in our lives. It's no wonder that Christians who have made mistakes leave the church, looking for help and support elsewhere, when the church is so unwilling to help. It took us weeks to get over our first church experience. In our conversations, we moaned and complained. We had to deal again with the bitterness that comes with rejection. The minister's words had done nothing to bring healing or help, it just caused our wounds to deepen. We never changed our life style and for a time we thought, "What's the point of trying to put things right with God?" and we rebelled even more. Have you ever been there?

Fortunately, God never gave up on us. Just because we had a bad church experience, it didn't change the Word of God or His calling and the conviction of the Holy Spirit. We still wanted to change and grow in our relationship with God. It was our move. What were we going to do? The book of James puts it this way:

> Therefore, submit to God. Resist the devil and he will flee from you. Draw near to God and He will draw near to you. Cleanse your hands you sinners; and purify your hearts, you double-minded. (James 4:7-8)

This scripture reveals this remarkable process. The first thing we had to do was submit to God and resist the devil. God wanted us in church, the devil wanted to keep us out. God kept reminding me of the benefits of being in church as it created a place for worship, hearing the Word, receiving from the Holy Spirit and receiving people's encouragement. The devil kept reminding me of our past church experience and told me that I should expect the same response next time. We had no choice; we had to submit to God, resist the devil and find another church.

Secondly, God wanted us to draw near to Him. God has promised us that He has made a way to Himself through Jesus and the Blood of the Lamb. We had to choose to walk towards Him to rekindle the relationship that He had initiated. He was calling us. We had to choose to listen and go the way He wanted us to go. Once we resisted the devil and started drawing near to God, we had the strength to do the third thing. We could finally cleanse our hands and deal with the sin in our lives, making the changes that we needed to bring us back into fellowship with God and his church.

Don't let past church experiences keep you out of church. It's where God wants you. You have a choice. You have to make the decision and get back on the path of recovery! Amanda and I decided to go to a smaller church, called Word of Life, in Bangor, Maine. The minister, Paul Warf and his wife Kim were great from the first day we entered the church. Going to this church was a step of faith and we knew many of the people in the fellowship. This meant they also knew us, and everything they had heard about us, yet they reached out to us in love. This church was what we had been looking for. It was small, intimate, with great worship, and the Word was delivered with power. There was space for the Holy Spirit to move. Everyone made us feel welcomed and it was not just words. They seemed genuine. After attending the church for a few weeks, both Amanda and I agreed this was where we felt the Lord was leading us. So, with the initial step made, it was time to speak to Paul, the minister.

This was a scary step of faith. I had trusted the last minister and was made to feel like a leper. I decided that I would not let this hold me back. I knew in my heart that I wanted to put everything right and move forward. The meeting with Paul was much more relaxed. We ate dinner and I told him all that had happened and again where Amanda and I were at, including the things we were still struggling with. I chose to be open and honest.

Paul's response was full of truth and grace. He first told me that we were more than welcome at the church. The doors were open for us to attend and that all that had happen in the past was behind us and we had to reach forward to the future. His grace was also mixed with reality and truth and in the same candor in which I had told him about the things that Amanda and I were still struggling with, he pointed me to the truth of the Word, encouraging us to make changes. He was not afraid to show love, but neither was he afraid to speak truth. This was the start of us truly repenting and changing.

What was different? What had changed? Why were we now willing to deal with our sin? All I can say is that unconditional love breaks every stronghold. Jesus gives an example of this in the book of Mark

> *Now the leper came to Him, imploring Him, kneeling down to Him and saying to Him, "If you are willing, You can make me clean"*
> *Then Jesus moved with compassion, stretched out His hand and touched him, and said to him, I am willing be cleansed"*
> *As soon as He had spoken, immediately the leprosy left him, and he was cleansed*
> *And He strictly warned him and sent him away at once*
> *And said to him, "See that you say nothing to anyone, but go your way, show yourself to the priest, and offer for your cleansing those things which Moses commanded, as a testimony to them".*
> *(Mark 1:40-44)*

When we read this, we need to understand the fate of a leper in those times. This man may have been a hard worker, living in the community, going to church (temple) and looking after his family. One day he wakes up, and the unthinkable happens. He has leprosy. It was something he never expected. Now that he had it, his leprosy would be considered judgment for a sinful life he had or because of the sins of his father. Overnight he would become an outcast and isolated to a camp of lepers. People wouldn't care how he got it or why. It was believed that in some way they had sinned against God and they were being punished. They are rejected and scorned and are required to leave everything that made up their life. This may seem very hard, and yet it's no different to the minister or individual who has suffered the trauma of a divorce whether through their own sin, or another's. They become an outcast.

In this scripture, the leper desperately risks all and comes to Jesus. Remember, if a leper were seen in public, they would be stoned because the people were afraid. They didn't want the leper's disease to touch them because they thought they would be afflicted with the disease. They did all they could to isolate the sin (the person) and keep them away from normal life. If they couldn't see them or come in contact with them they didn't have to deal with them! Does this sound like a church near you?

Jesus' response is breathtaking. Imagine the scene. Everything goes into slow motion as the leper approaches Jesus and starts *"imploring Him"*. The disciples are aghast, turning round and wondering what will happen. They begin "screaming and shouting, get away". They are afraid that the leper will touch Jesus and He will be affected with this disease. And then with a smile, Jesus caused the minds and feelings of the disciples to go into a spin as He *"reached out and touched him"*, the leper. Time and space freezes in the eyes of the disciples, "What has Jesus done?" And then, Jesus says, *"I am willing, be cleansed."*

It's this kind of ministry that makes us fall more and more in love with Jesus. He doesn't do what you or I would do. He refuses to run from this potential religious disaster. He is moved with compassion and compelled to bring a kingdom perspective through kingdom actions. Before Jesus healed him, He touched him. What would this have done in the leper's heart? Maybe for the first time in years, the leper had human contact! Jesus' acceptance and love for this outcast made it possible for him to receive his miracle. Jesus didn't want him to stay in a state of being afflicted by leprosy. He demonstrated his words, *"I am willing,"* with an action of acceptance. Jesus wanted him to know that he was loved, even before he was changed. Acceptance, Isn't that something we are all looking for, especially when we have messed things up? We need someone standing in our corner saying "you messed that one up, now let's clean it up and get things back on track".

The story gets better. We discover that the leper isn't a sinner, or Gentile, but a Jew. We know this because Jesus sent him to the priest to offer a sacrifice. How would he have known what sacrifice he had to make if he wasn't a Jew? If this account was written today it could be any Christian who has had an experience that has left them isolated from church. This could be a person who has sinned, or has some kind of sickness, or dresses in a way that is not becoming in the church. They become an outcast. They don't fit the mold, and for whatever reason, they feel like they have been driven out of church. These are the kind of people Jesus has come for. Wasn't it Jesus that said, *"I have not come for the righteous,"* (Matthew 9:13) nor should we say the perfect, holy Christian? Jesus came to shake hands with the sinner, embrace the prostitute, and have dinner with thieving tax collectors. He was never afflicted by their sin, but they were drastically changed by His grace

For me, Paul Warf was like Jesus to the leper. He reached out to Amanda and me and accepted us for who we were. The things that we had struggled to come to terms with and change over the past few months we could now face and we had the strength to make changes. Someone believed in us and they were willing to walk with us through the journey of repentance and restoration. This act of acceptance was enough to pull down the walls of rejection we had built around our hearts and allow God to start changing our lives.

It takes a strong, radical minister to stand by people who have fallen. I am not sure if Pastor Paul knew that day when he welcomed us to the church, the questions he would be asked, or the people who would come against him for having us in his church. He would have to stand tall and he did. There were times when other people never realized the repentance we had gone through or the changes we had made in our lives, but Paul and Kim did, and they stood by us. The day we started going to Word of Life church was a new day for us. Everything changed and we entered an environment in which we could change and be re-molded by God. God wanted us back in church and that's where He got us.

When a person goes through difficult situations as Christians they are left feeling wounded. God has to bring correction in those moments. When God puts His finger on the things in our lives, He wants us to change and the wounds seem to deepen. It's like putting salt on open flesh. However, God touched those painful areas in our lives, and started the healing process.

Being rebuked or corrected is never easy. Think about how a good parent corrects their children. There may be some strong words, some advice, and direction, but then they throw their arms around them to show them how much they love them. It's in this safe environment that correction can be successfully ministered. That's how I see the church dealing with a fallen saint or minister. God wants to bring correction, but He wants to do it in a safe, loving environment. The church is meant to be that place. The church is the extension of God's arms. It is to be a place of grace and truth, of love and correction.

I have known other ministers who have faced difficult situations and felt like the leper in the church. Afraid of what people might think or say, they have chosen to stay away from church and today they remain in a place of bitterness. They will talk about Jesus, ministry and church life, but it's all in the past tense. They talk about what used to be and what they used to do. They have no vision for today and no dreams for tomorrow. They are stuck in the past and they will remain in that place until they decide to let Jesus heal their wounds. They will tell you that they can have Jesus in their homes and that they pray every day but they refuse to allow the arms of God to embrace them. I am so grateful that we listened to the prompting of the Holy Spirit and even though the job of finding the right church wasn't without pain, when we found it, we found the love and grace of God. We will be forever indebted to Pastor Paul and Kim of Word of Life church. As God continues to restore and use us, they will know that they have a part in our ministry.

Chapter 6
TEAR, TEARS MORE TEARS THEN JOY!

From the moment Amanda and I started attending Word of Life church, we not only came face to face with Jesus, but with ourselves. The decision we had made, the images of the people we had hurt, and the sins we had committed came clearly into focus. Just when we thought the tears were going to stop, they got worse. I remember complaining to Amanda that I was tired of crying and wanted to stop, but I couldn't. God had a hold of my heart.

I thought church was a place to feel good, but for a season, I felt worse by going to church. I believe this is why many people don't stick it out... they run. It reminded me of when I was a young boy when I started going to the youth club at the local church. I enjoyed the club, but to be a part of it, you had to attend the church on Sunday. I tried it for a few weeks, but every time I went, I left with more questions than answers, more fears than faith. It made me think about God, heaven and hell and things that I didn't want to come face to face with at the age of ten. So I left! I never went back to church again until I made a decision for Jesus at the age of fifteen. Then, at thirty-six, I found myself in the same place! When I went to church, it created questions I didn't want to answer, so I was left with a choice, should I stay or should I go? The deciding factor for me was that I really wanted Jesus in my life, and I didn't want to waste another five years trying to hide from an omnipresent God!

Everyone at some point in their life wants to run and hide. It's easier than dealing with truth and that's how I felt at this point in my life. I wanted God, but I didn't always want to hear what He had to say because I knew it would require some changes in my life. Once in church, the barriers slowly came down and I came face to face with Jesus again. It was time for repentance.

I have to say I had no intention of writing a chapter that deals with repentance because it's different for everyone. Repentance is a journey, with many questions, tears and decisions. I wish I could have titled this chapter "The day I repented" and been able to give you the ten steps of putting everything right, but that's impossible. Repentance is not a one-time experience. It is an ongoing process of discovering the mistakes we have made and dealing with them. I have learned that God doesn't deal with all our issues at one time. He puts His finger on a particular problem, operates on it and treats it until it is healed. Then, he starts on the next problem. We tend to know the obvious mistakes but we come to realize that the actions we make are surrounded by thoughts and beliefs that we have held onto for a long time, and they are not always godly. In repenting, we have to deal with all our thoughts and come face to face with our belief system. We need to hold onto that which is godly and let go of what causes us to stray from righteous living.

I hope that by sharing the process in which I repented, and what God brought me through, it will help others to deal with the mistakes they have made in their past and move on. In talking about my experience, I have to share what the scriptures say. From the moment I had become a Christian I fell in love with the Word and I believe it to be truth. As a preacher, it was always in my hand, on my desk or being spoken through my mouth. When I resigned from my position as pastor, I also decided to take a break from the Bible. It was not intentional, but I just didn't pick it up. I knew what it said but I didn't want to go there. Yes, I realize it was a bad move!

The first thing God restored in my Life when I started to repent was the Word of God. It wasn't easy to pick it up, because the Word is like a mirror and when we look at it, it reflects who we are and where we are in our life. However, it is also a light in the darkness. It is like a road map. The Word of God is the navigating tool that brings us out of the dark terrain of the wilderness, and brings us back into the Promised Land. As I started to repent and come to terms with my sin, God led me to Psalm 51. This became a source of instruction and encouragement. King David wrote this psalm or song after he had sinned, by looking at another man's wife bathing on a rooftop. David decided he wanted that which was not his to have. He made his decision and went after her. It wasn't long before they were sleeping together and she got pregnant. Imagine the panic in David's heart! He was the anointed King of Israel, and he had got another man's wife pregnant! How was he going to get out of this mess? *(2 Samuel 11)*

David's first solution was to try to get her husband, Uriah, to leave the battlefield and sleep with his wife. He thought his "clever" plan would disguise his sin. Unfortunately for David, Uriah was too loyal to the king and he didn't feel it was right to go home while the Ark was in a Tent and his fellow solders were in a battlefield. David went back to the drawing board and came up with another plan. He decided to have Uriah sent to the forefront of the hottest battle and have his other men retreat. Leaving Uriah to face the enemy on his own and meet certain death. David easily discarded Uriah's life in an effort to hide his own sin. The king became a murderer as well as an adulterer! *(2 Samuel 11)*

David, in his pride, didn't think much of about his sin. He didn't repent immediately. He tried to forget about it and cover it up. It was only when he was approached by the Prophet Nathan, who exposed his sin, that David repented and experienced God's forgiveness. *(2 Samuel 12:13)* It's interesting that we try to cover our sin, but only God can take it away! As long as we hold on to it, there is no peace, just torment. The moment we give it to God and truly repent, peace and joy are restored. It's hard to see the process that David went through in this portion of scripture, but when we look at Psalm 51, we can clearly see the journey he went through. It is a journey we all can relate to:

Have mercy upon me, O God,
According to your loving kindness,

According to the multitude of your tender mercies,
Blot out my transgressions,
Wash me thoroughly from my iniquity,
And cleanse me from my sin.
(Psalm 51:1-2)

David caught hold of the great truth, that God is full of mercy. Because of this revelation, he was able to go before God and ask Him for forgiveness. Have you ever said you are sorry to someone that is unforgiving? You are left with a feeling of never wanting to apologize to that person again, no matter what you do wrong. Well, the opposite is true when you have a God encounter which is full of grace and forgiveness. You know that even though God may be disappointed and that He may have a few choice words of correction, He will still love you and help you move on.

This psalm is a great picture of a God that wants to forgive us. It reflects His heart towards us. The attributes we see are the same that caused God the Father to send His only begotten Son, Jesus to die on the cross and shed his blood for our sin. This Psalm foreshadows the grace of God seen in the life of Jesus and his ability to forgive. Peter once questioned Jesus about this very subject and how many times a person should forgive a sinning brother. Peter thought, he had it wrapped up when he said *"Should you forgive him seven times?"* Peter restricted God's mercy. Jesus blew him out of the water when He replied and said we should forgive *"seventy times seven, a day."* Peter couldn't fathom the extent of the mercy and grace of God at that time, but I'm sure Jesus' words were ringing through his heart when he sinned by denying Jesus just before the crucifixion. *(Matthew 18:21-21)*

When we repent we cry for different reasons. Obviously, we have caused pain to others. Another reason for tears is when we face the consequences of the decisions we have made. We could call this, self-pity. These are the worse kind of tears! Then there are the tears of healing, when we realize how mercifully and gracious our heavenly Father is. It causes us to want to run into His arms and tell Him how sorry we are, as we stand in awe and amazement at His love for us. This is the love, grace and mercy that we have trouble comprehending, because it's not of this world. Mankind fails to exhibit this kind of mercy, so they become judgmental. However, once we catch it, once we see and experience it, we never treat people the same. It changes who we are for the better.

Some ministers are afraid that if people understand the greatness of God's mercy, it will cause their congregation to sin more. So, instead of grace, they preach judgment. However, when we really understand this revelation, it causes us to sin less as we fall more and more in love with Jesus. We desire to do what's right and steer away from that which is wrong. It was on this foundation that David approached God and repented. David used three different words to describe the mistakes he made, transgression, iniquity and sin. Many people think these are all the same, but that is far from the truth.

The first word David uses is *"transgressions"* which means rebellion or a premeditated act of sin. The second word is *"iniquity"*, which means crooked or perverted. It is used in reference to the wickedness in the heart of man that causes him to love sin and walk in the ways of the world. Finally, he uses the word *"sin"* which means to miss the mark. It is sin when we do something we didn't intend or plan to do, it just happened!

David's repentance started with a confession that he wanted God to forgive him for his transgressions or his direct rebellion against the will of God. In saying this, he acknowledged that he had decided to rebel and do things his way. He knew what he was doing, it was premeditated and wrong, yet he still chose to do it. This scripture helped me a great deal. Like everyone else, I have sinned and missed the mark. However, in making some of the decisions I made, and in getting a divorce, I knew it was against God's Word and I still did it. We don't like to admit our mistakes, but the truth remains that it was direct rebellion. I thought I knew best and I didn't see any other way of moving forward. Obviously, God knows best. He knows the heartache of divorce. He knows the pain and grief it would cause everyone involved and He wanted to avoid it at all cost. However, we can't change what we did yesterday, and it was the decision I had made.

I have repented many times for sins, but to face God with open rebellion is hard. Why would He want to forgive me? Why should He? Well, He doesn't have to, but to be merciful is part of who God is. We have to be truthful with ourselves to be truly honest in our repentance before God. It was no one else's mistake. I made a decision and it was wrong. When you finally get past that part, you will find the mercy of God flood your heart and the tears of grief and pain will be turned into tears of healing.

Through years in ministry, I have counseled and seen many people who have gone through divorce. There are those who are honest and confess their mistakes, truly repenting. I have seen them restored and they move on with their lives with great blessing. At the same time, I have seen other people who have repented with their lips, but have never actually accepted that they had rebelled against God and made mistakes. They seem to get stuck in the "divorced and bitter group" and never move forward. There is a way to restoration but we have to be honest before God.

The second thing we see here in verse 2, is that David seems to get a New Testament revelation. He doesn't ask for his sins to be covered or atoned for in Old Testament pattern. He asks that his sin be "blotted out" as thought it never existed, and removed from his life that he may be cleansed. We will never really understand what it is to be cleansed unless we accept that God has dealt with our sin and that it has been blotted out David reiterates this when he writes Psalm 103:12. When God deals with sin, David declares that God remembers our sin no more:

As far as the east is from the west, So far has He removed our transgression (Premeditated rebellion) from us. (Psalm 103:12)

If David could get this revelation about God's mercy under the old covenant, how much more should we walk in this truth when we realize the price that Jesus paid for us when He died on the cross. He has dealt with our sin. We are righteous and have been made holy, not by our own good works, but through Christ's sacrifice. He knew we would fail and make mistakes and He paid a price for us through the shedding of His blood before we ever sinned. This doesn't mean we can just do what we want, but when we make mistakes, even premeditated ones, we have an advocate in Christ. We still have to repent and change our ways but the blood still speaks. To suggest that we will remain in an unforgiven state or even to believe words of judgment and condemnation from others is to say that our sin is more powerful than Christ's sacrifice and His power to forgive.

We have to remember that conviction comes from God. He convicts us of our sins. Condemnation is from the devil. *(Romans 8)* The devil desires to chain our minds and hearts by reminding us of our mistakes, keeping us bound. He may even use Christians to attack us. We need to remember that our fight *"is not against flesh and blood but against principalities and power" (Ephesians 6:12)*. The devil is the accuser of the brethren and he wants to turn brothers against brothers to see the kingdom of God divided and fighting against itself. *(Revelation 12:10)* Jesus came to set the captives free, to forgive and cleanse us from the stench of sin and to give us the power to live freely. We experience this power when we accept His forgiveness.

Continuing with Psalm 51, brings more balance and insight:

For I acknowledge my transgressions, and my sin is always before me. (Psalm 51:3)

Although this may sound like a contradiction, David is actually giving us a full picture of the consequence of sin. He has already asked God to "blot out" his transgression and to "cleanse him". This is work that only God can do and it is complete. In His work, the barrier of sin that separates us in our relationship from God is removed and we are restored to our rightful place. However, David also recognizes that there are short and long-term consequences for the errors he has made. No matter how much God has forgiven him, there are still life issues that he needs to deal with. He made the decision to have Bathsheba's husband killed. This will affect his family members and the warriors with whom he served. The next time someone is sent to battle and placed on the front line, they will wonder about the king's motives. David's example to his children is marred, and respect lost. David's sin had many effects.

The Bible is clear when it states:

> "Do not be deceived (don't kid yourself), God is not mocked, for what so ever a man sows, that he will also reap" (Galatians 6:7).

The law of sowing and reaping is both spiritual and natural. Whatever you put your time, effort and energy into, you will benefit from it. If we sow into the flesh or our own desires, the effects are not only felt by us, but by everyone we have contact with.

This is one of the hardest things to come to terms with when there is a divorce, regardless of who initiated the decision. I know that I'm forgiven, and that my sins are blotted out, but that doesn't stop the pain that occurs when I think of the people I have hurt. I have cried for others and their pain, more than I have cried for myself. There were people who looked to me as an example, and I disappointed them. Yes, they can and do forgive, but the weeks and months of pain and questioning I caused in their hearts can never be taken away.

When you go through a divorce, parents are affected. They have always wanted the best for their children and they are suddenly faced not only with the pain their child is going through, but also the pain of loosing someone that has become part of the family. Your ex, becomes their ex. Children also get caught in the middle of the pain. They never ask for their parents to get divorced. Some suffer in silence, while others may become very angry, but all are affected. Everyday activities change such as where they are living, who takes them to school, holiday events, vacations - everything changes. Our choice will cause them to always be part of a broken family.

Some marriages are a nightmare for the kids. When there is continuous arguing or various types of abuse, these relationships are an unhealthy environment for children. In such cases, the benefits of change may outweigh the pain. However, the fact remains, our choices or sins, have an effect that continues to live with us. The good news is that God can and does intervene, if we let Him. We have a responsibility to try to mend broken relationships, and to pray for those we have hurt. We are to ask God to give us wisdom with our children and do all we can to right the wrongs we have made. We have to gain respect again by making more right decisions in the future, to overcome the poor choices from the past. Broken families become blended families and we have a new opportunity to be a godly example.

We need to try and understand other people's pain. When people are angry and reject you, we need to respond with love. That may manifest itself in the decision not to let bitterness gain control of your mind. It may be seen in a letter of repentance, time in prayer, or with children, continuous love and affection. I have found in my own journey that some people continue to struggle with the mistakes I have made. They will not let go of them and they continue to hold a grudge or walk in judgment. My choice to forgive them, is a continual one, with the hope that they one day will be able to forgive me for my sins. There will always be people that are ready to remind or punish us for our past. We have to understand our present position in Christ, as forgiven, and as He has forgiven us many times, we should continue to forgive others.

I have faced all of the above. Due to my sin, and people being hurt, I had to apologize to them and display a repentant heart. There were times I did this in person. When that wasn't possible, I wrote a letter or sent an email. It is impossible to repent without some kind of action or demonstration of that repentance. This verse clearly states, *"I acknowledge my transgressions…."* We have to realize what we have done and in whatever manner we repent, it should be seen in our actions towards others. When we take this step, our burden will be lifted. There were times that God brought me to a place of acknowledging the pain I had caused Laura. We were past the point of having reconciliation in our marriage, but I still had to express my sorrow and repent before her. I am thankful that she accepted my repentance and chose to forgive me.

God also convicted me of the pain, disappointment and questioning my actions had created in the minds of other pastors who I had released into ministry, and within the leaders of the churches I had overseen in England. I had no option but to express my sorrow for my mistakes and the pain I had caused them, when I should have set a better example. There are times however, when we are no longer in a position to speak to some people personally. In these situations, all we can do is pray for them. We have to trust that God will minister to their hearts. All I know is, that where there is true repentance, it requires more than just words of sorrow before God, it requires action.

As I took these steps and added actions to the repentance in my heart, the burden of pain I had been feeling began to lift. There was a temptation to keep writing, emailing and apologizing. What started out as a godly act of humility can turn into a need to make we feel better. However, there comes a point when we need to accept that we have done all we can, and it is time to *"forget those things which are behind and reaching forward to those things which are ahead." (Philippians 3:13)* As we experience all these emotions, the forgiveness and sorrow, we are brought to a point of decision.

How will we live the rest of our lives? Will we continue to live under a cloud of depression, or will we choose to move forward. It is impossible to change our yesterday, but the right decisions we make today, will change our tomorrow. God makes it possible, but we have to walk it out, live in the peace He has given, and accept the righteousness He has clothed us with.

King David sings about repentance and forgiveness and then suddenly he speaks of being purged with hyssop. What does hyssop have to do with repentance and moving on with our lives?

> *"Purge me with Hyssop and I will be clean; Wash me and I will be whiter than snow."(Psalm 51:7)*

David understood how God dealt with His people, and he used it in this Psalm as a declaration of faith. In the Old Testament, we read of God rescuing Israel out of the hand of Pharaoh who had held them against their will in Egypt. They had become slaves to that nation, and when they tried to leave, they were punished by Pharaoh. God responded to Egypt's dictatorship by sending ten plagues. We need to explore in more detail, the final plague to understand the significance of "Hyssop" and how it applies to us in repentance.

God made a declaration through Moses that if Pharaoh did not release the Children of Israel to worship their God, then the first-born male of every family in the land would perish. The exception to this would be for those who applied the blood of a lamb to the doorposts and lintel of their home, the child would be saved. The method of applying the blood was through hyssop. *(Exodus 12)* To the Children of Israel, hyssop represented their faith. They believed what God said and the promise He had made. They believed in the power of the blood and the safety that would come to them if they acted on faith, and dipping the hyssop into the blood and sprinkling it on their doorpost and door lintel. We know their faith was rewarded with deliverance. King David used this analogy as he struggled to come to terms with his sin and the choices he had made. In his song of repentance, he used the word "hyssop" to declare that he had made a faith decision to believe God's promise and on that basis, he asked and received forgiveness.

As Christians, we have a greater promise that was delivered to us through Jesus. Not only was He the messenger sent from the Father, but He was also the Lamb of God that was without blemish or sin. He became our sacrifice, shedding His blood that we could be forgiven. *(John 1:36)* Now, we are faced with a faith decision. Do we believe the promise of God over our feelings and self-pity? Do we believe that God's grace is more powerful than our sins? Do we believe that God wants the best for us despite our poor decisions? Will we allow God to deliver us from the burden of our rebellion?

Forgiveness and moving forward is not easy. We tend to struggle with letting go of our sins more than other people do. We have to make a faith decision to move on. Without faith in God, and His ability to cause us to move on with our lives, we become enslaved by our past mistakes. We are trapped in a time zone of yesterday with no hope of future happiness. When we apply faith, instead of feelings, we demonstrate a total dependency on God's ability and desire to forgive, allowing us to move forward with our lives. When faith is applied, the heavens stop feeling like brass. We can come again to the throne of grace with boldness *(Hebrews 10:19-25)*, with confidence that God wants to hear our prayers and answer them. We regain the faith that God has a plan and purpose for our lives. By making a faith decision, our concept of God and the world changes for the better. We re-engage with the plans and purposes of God, knowing that God wants to use us.

As King David made a stand based on his faith he expected a breakthrough. He went on to write in this Psalm *"Make me hear joy and gladness, that the bones you have broken may rejoice"*. *(Psalm 51:8)* Our faith in God's grace causes the dark days of despair to disappear and we can laugh and be happy again. For me, this took time. I found myself walking around in self-pity, not knowing how to be in public or what to say to people. I didn't even realize that the shame of divorce had overtaken me. Once I applied faith and accepted forgiveness, God started to give me a new perspective of myself. My confidence and joy returned. That which was broken, began to be healed as I rediscovered who I was in Christ Jesus. When I made a decision to accept God's forgiveness by faith, everything started to change for the better. Although my future was still filled with questions, I knew that God had a plan. He would lead me by the hand into His purpose and my destiny.

The great thing about true repentance is that when you are restored, you become a better individual because you have a better understanding of God's love and grace. Your heart is changed and God remolds and reshapes it. This is what I think David is talking about in the next part of this wonderful psalm:

> "Create in me a clean heart, O God.
> And renew a steadfast spirit in me" (Psalm 51:10)

This is something we have all prayed for at some point in our lives. We have all cried out in pain, with tears and great desire, saying "Change me God; create in me a clean heart". It's a prayer that says we are done with the old self and the mistakes we have made and that we want to change. It's also a realization that we have an inability to change on our own and we need a heart transplant. God needs to intervene and help us change the way we think and act. We need God to reshape us. We are drawn to the illustration from Jeremiah 18, where God sends the prophet to the potter's house. There, he sees the potter (God) take the clay vessel which is marred in some way, and the creator's hands start to reshapes the vessel until he is happy with it. We know that God is speaking about the nation Israel and His desire to take them with all their rebellion and reshape them into vessels of great honor.

In the same way that God wanted to restore and reshape Israel, so God wants to take us, with all our mistakes and carefully shape us, molding us and creating a heart in us that He desires. He wants us to become vessels of great honor again, useful in His hands. The picture of the potter and the clay gives us a kingdom image of the heart of God. It's an image that may seem foreign to us, and unbelievable to others who look on. We have all said, "that person will never change." We have all judged and condemned someone, yet God sees the potential and, if we let Him, He will mold us into the vessels He wants us to be.

As David calls on God to intervene and re-create a new heart, he also asks that God will give him the ability to renew his steadfast spirit. There was a time when David did not struggle as much with his sin, and desired only to walk in the ways of God. This is also true of us. We have all had that righteous indignation that wants to walk right. Not only do we need a recreated heart, we need to be steadfast again in our walk. We have to make a decision to stop being double minded. We need to stop walking by the Spirit one day, and in the flesh another day. We have to endeavor to always walk in and by the Spirit *(Galatians 5:16)*.

The next part of this Psalm is the section that reflects my heart the most.

> *"Do not cast me away from Your presence,*
> *And do not take Your Holy Spirit from me*
> *Restore to me the joy or Your salvation*
> *And uphold me by your generous Spirit"*
> *(Psalm 51:11-12)*

When I made a decision for Jesus, I started going to a church that was open to the working of the Holy Spirit. The church believed in the supernatural. Miracles and manifestation where part of the Christian norm! We knew our salvation came through accepting Jesus as Lord and Savior but we also understood that the Father had sent another Helper, the Holy Spirit to lead and direct us in the things of God. *(John 14)*.

The presence of the Holy Spirit has always been very real in my life, and I have always relied on His anointing to do the things that God had called me to. I have always been open to the direction and guidance of the Holy Spirit in ministry and life. I heard His voice very clearly and it's very important to me to be directed by the Spirit

When I went through my divorce, my greatest fear was that I would lose my relationship with God and not experience the presence of the Holy Spirit or hear His voice ever again. When I first resigned from my pastoral positions in the church in Maine, as I made my own decisions, it became harder to hear the voice of the Holy Spirit. This was not because He wasn't talking, but because I had stopped listening. I soon realized, that I had taken a step backward in my relationship with God, and not hearing His voice or feeling His presence became very difficult for me. It led me to a time of crying out and begging God to speak to me. This Psalm came into my mind all the time, and I would beg God not to take His presence from me. I knew I needed the Holy Spirit. I needed God more at this time in my life than ever before. I also realized that I needed to change my attitude and come to a place where I would yield myself before God and start living how He wanted me to live.

This struggle continued until Amanda and I started going to Word of Life. When we started yielding our lives to God again, I started to feel God's presence again and hear His voice. It started on the second Sunday we were in the church. There was a call for ministry and even though I didn't want to be prayed for, I wanted the presence of God. My Spirit was hungry for Him, yet my flesh wanted to go home and have lunch. Finally I submitted to the Spirit and went for prayer. The presence of God filled me immediately and it was as if as He had never left. The next few times

I went to church, I would get into the worship, feel the presence of God and start crying. I slowly started to realize that I had walked away from God. I went through the process of complaining to God about what others had done to me and how they had influenced me, causing me to make the decisions I had made. However, it didn't take long for me to accept that I had made the decisions that were impacting my life and I needed to repent.

My desire for the presence of the Holy Spirit and my hunger to hear His voice went beyond a church service. I found myself at home and on my own everyday. I chose to use this time to call out to God. There in the bedroom or living room I would cry out to be touched by the Holy Spirit and I would feel the presence of God filling the place. His glory would be so strong in the room that I would not be able to stand. With the presence of God filling me, I found myself submitting more and more and starting to change. Some days I would just feel God's love and His peace would consume me. There was the assurance that He was with me and that He would never leave me. Other days, there would be great conviction and I would find myself crying out for forgiveness. During this season of fresh outpouring and infilling, I felt my spirit man becoming stronger and stronger. He enabled me to cope with the day, to deal with the past, and to look forward with hope. With every prayer and outpouring of the Holy Spirit, God would speak to me through the scriptures. I always felt encouraged. I was armed with the Word and no matter what difficulties I would face, I knew God had spoken to me.

When we are in a place where we are struggling with the flesh or decisions we have made, we need to get prayer, ministry or just begin calling out to God for His presence to fill us. When we get into the presence of God, we start changing. It was in this place, that God *"restored the joy of my salvation"*. I was excited to be a Christian again! The trial of the year was disappearing; God was flooding my heart and life with His light. His presence changed everything. I, like King David, made the same request of our heavenly

Father, requesting that He would *"Uphold me with your generous Spirit."* David caught an aspect of God's grace and mercy. He realized that God didn't want to give us a minimum dose of His presence, but a maximum outpouring. How much do you want Him? How much can you take? He will fill you to your hearts desire.

When the Spirit of God moves upon us it causes a reaction. We can't contain it so we have to give it away. The result of God creating a new heart in King David, and in him receiving the presence of God, brought about restoration of joy and a passion to teach others the things of God

> *"Then I will teach transgressors your ways and sinners shall be converted to you."* (Psalm 51:13)

Look at the transformation that has taken place through repentance. King David has gone from confessing his sins and transgression, to a place of being recreated by God and desiring to teach other sinners the ways of God. The Bible says that *"freely we have received, freely give."* (Matthew 10:8) When we receive from God, we want to give it to others. We can't contain all of His grace and love. We need to give it away. We have made mistakes, and now have knowledge and experience of God's power. If we can forgive ourselves and get beyond what others think, we can become a great tool in God's hands.

God spoke to me about this process and told me that I didn't have one great testimony of salvation but two testimony of His grace. I can speak from experience of His salvation and His restoration. I have a choice whether I let my past decisions cloud me in guilt, and become powerless in the hands of God, or I can choose to accept God's forgiveness and walk a life of faith, using my life experience as a vehicle to help others. The repentance and restoration God has brought me through is now a tool in God's hands. The enemy wanted to destroy my life and the ministry God had called me to. Through submission to God, that which the enemy tried to use to destroy my life has become a weapon for the kingdom of God.

I can now overcome the enemy in the lives of others breaking the stronghold of guilt, fear, doubt and unforgiveness through the power of the Blood of the Lamb and the words of my testimony:

> And they overcame him (devil) by the blood of the lamb and by the word of their testimony" (Revelation 12:11)

Don't you just love it when you know you're on the winning side?

I want to conclude this chapter by declaring God's desire to bring us to a point of repentance that brings change and restoration. God is not looking for empty words of sorrow or the tears of self-pity because we have been found out or humbled by our experience. God is not looking for more money or weekly visits to the homeless shelter to help others in an effort of covering our guilt and shame as we try to prove our love to God. King David said:

> "For you do not desire sacrifices,
> Or else I would give it,
> You do not delight in burnt offering,
> The sacrifice of God is a broken spirit,
> A broken and contrite heart
> These O God, You will not despise.
> (Psalm 51:16-17)

God wants true brokenness, where we truly examine our hearts, and repent of the sins we have committed. God want us to be willing to yield all and give ourselves to Him. God will not reject that person, but restores them to the place He has desired for them. As I stated at the beginning of this chapter, the process of repenting and restoration doesn't happen in a day, or a week. It takes time; it's a journey. For me it started when I made a decision to go back to church. I never let the religious people stop me. I was willing to press through beyond my own pride. I endured the way people looked at me, their questions, and the doubts in my own mind. I found a place where Jesus loves the leper, and He is willing and He continues to heal the broken and restore our lives.

As I came to this place, and experienced God restoring my spiritual man, I found it easier to move on and find God in other areas of my life. There were still many questions and a journey before me but I had truly repented and the road to restoration had begun.

Chapter 7
MANNA FROM HEAVEN

One of the most awesome things about God, is that He is steadfast. He never changes His character or His love towards us. When He makes a promise, He keeps it. I am not sure if any of these things can be said about us as we change depending on how we feel or what we desire. The love we show others often fluctuates as it is usually based on the love or respect we receive. We try to keep the promises we have made, yet we've all had those moments when we have made promises, and due to circumstances, we were unable to keep them. No matter how trustworthy we try to be, we will fail and let other people down. Thankfully, God is who and what He says He is. The Bible clearly states that Jesus is the *"same yesterday, today and forever"*. *(Hebrews 13:8)* Just because we change the way we live, doesn't change who God is. It's hard to believe, but God is holy and faithful all of the time.

One thing that I experienced when I went through my divorce was the experience of a wilderness season. There were people who abandoned me. I experienced times of loneliness and questioning that made me feel as if the whole world had changed towards me. When I prayed I felt as if my prayers were hitting the ceiling and I wondered if God was still out there. Even if God was still there, I questioned if He cared about me. For those who have also experienced this wilderness, we need to remember the good news is that God does care and He still reaches out to us. Moses told the Children of Israel, that they were to be careful in their walk before God and not stray from doing the right thing. Then he told them, that when they did the wrong thing, which he knew they would, God would still be there for them.

> *"(For the Lord your God is a merciful God), He will not forsake you nor destroy you, nor forget the covenant (promise) of your fathers which he swore (promised) them. (Deuteronomy 4:31)*

No matter what mistakes we have made or where we are in our wilderness experience, God has not changed. He is still there even when we find that concept hard to believe. If people treated us with the same contempt and lack of integrity with which we treat God, we would have nothing to do with them. God is truly a God of mercy.

When Israel was in their wilderness experience they quickly forgot the miracles of deliverance, complained and became bitter. God rescued them, and gave them sweet water to drink. In Exodus 16, we read that God provided food for them every day. This provision from heaven was called manna or "angel food". The people were told to go out everyday and collect the manna. They were not to save any of it but trust that God would provide for them the next day supply. He continued this every day until their wilderness journey was over and they came to the Promised Land. *(Joshua 5:12)* God wanted to increase their faith for provision and teach them not to trust in their own ability, or understanding but to trust in God's provision. Whenever we go through a wilderness experience, there is always something that causes us to call on God. He creates a Godly dependency. If we learn the lesson of dependence on God, and do away with our spirit of independence, we will strengthen our faith and this will rekindle our relationship with the Father. He wants us to trust Him, He wants to us to draw near to Him. And He wants us to know that He doesn't change. Even when we make mistakes, we can continue to trust in Him.

This was a very real experience for Amanda and me. We were in the midst of facing the world with our relationship, repenting for the wrongs we had done and we had both gone through a divorce. We were feeling very low. We were going to church again, yet we faced judgmental words, attitudes, and lies that quickly spread through the church's "grapevine." In addition to this, we struggled with not being in the ministry. We were left wondering where God was, and if He still loved us. In the midst of all this, we had very real financial needs. We had to call on God to intervene, as we had no natural way of making it through the mess we had created.

This was a major obstacle to us and we felt we needed enough faith to move mountains. It's a good thing God only required a faith the size of a mustard seed as that was about all we could come up with! *(Matthew 17:20)* One of the areas that God had always proved faithful in my life was through finances. Not that I always had abundance, but I had never gone without. I believed, and still do, in the giving of tithes and offerings to the local church and trusting God to provide my needs, He has never failed.

Over the years I have seen God provide in miraculous ways. People have just given me money at crucial times or checks would appear in the mail. However, most of the time, gifts had been given through people in my congregation who believed that God was leading them. Without sounding cynical, there are some people who give because God leads them, and there are others who give because you are the pastor and they want to be your "friend" or part of a particular ministry. Yet, with every gift I have ever received, they were always given at the time of my need and I was grateful for them, but there were still times when I questioned the motive of the giver.

Having faith for provision had been easy for me in the past when I was in ministry, but what would happen now? I was not ministering, or leading a church. I wasn't seen as the safe investment and my walk before God was somewhat marred. I didn't have a network of people to rely on and I questioned if God would want to answer my need for provision. As I have said, I had resigned from my pastor position and I was unable to work due to visa restrictions. I had already returned to the UK once, to have my visa changed, but it was still restricted to working in the ministry. I was not yet in a place where God was leading me to minister to others as He was still restoring me. Amanda was working, but her income could not cover the cost of looking after herself, the children and supporting two homes.

Through my adult life, I had made godly choices in my finances. I have never been in debt. I didn't buy what I couldn't afford and I was always able to save money. The financial choices I had made in the past, kept me going through the first part of my wilderness experience. However, the resources were running out and we needed God to intervene. I believe God allowed us to get to this place of need because it created a dependency on Him. It caused us to activate our faith, and to discover God's faithfulness in the midst of the mess we had created.

The first check that appeared in the mail was awesome, and a true sign that God had heard our hearts cry and we knew He was still with us. Our faith for this provision wasn't released through a mighty prayer but by a conversation Amanda and I had in the car. I forget where we were going but we were talking about the financial needs we had, and the stress it was causing us. This was a new place for me, and I started sharing with Amanda about how God had always met my needs with "miracle money". To put this in context, I'm not a "name it, claim it, blab it, grab it, kind of guy," I just believe that God said He would provide! As we were talking, the question that filled our hearts was whether God would do for us now, considering the choices we had made? It was in that moment that a glimmer of faith touched my heart. The next second, I was telling Amanda that God would provide for us because of His love for us, and that we would find a check in the mail. Our words have the power of life *(Proverbs 18:21)* and even though we didn't pray, God could see our hearts. *(Matthew 6:8)*

When God sees faith, no matter how small, He moves. The next day, I checked the mail with the expectation of faith, and God did not disappoint me. There was a check in the mail from someone I had never met or spoken to, with a note that said God had led her to send the money. I couldn't wait to call Amanda and tell her. She was so excited, I could hear the relief and joy as she told me that God had never done that for her before. It is so awesome when God moves! The money was a welcome relief, but what it did was more than pay a few bills. First, it revealed that God is faithful and loving. Even though we had made some big mistakes, God never changes. Second, it gave us faith to ask again. The check we received helped us through that month, but it would not sustain our needs for the months to come. God could have sent a larger check to keep us going for the duration of our journey, but that would not have developed our faith and dependency on Him in the way that He intended. We may be in a wilderness, but we are never alone. We need to throw ourselves on God's mercy and He will prove faithful!

The process of trusting and asking God to provide manna from heaven didn't happen once, but time and time again over the next year. Whenever we had a major need, we called out and God answered. Again, for the cynically-minded, as we have all been, to pray and receive a check once could be coincidence, but for it to happen time and time again is miraculous. The good news is that we serve a God that loves to demonstrate His Kingdom power and move the mountains in our life.

During this time, God wanted to deal with an area of pride in my life. From a young age, I believed it was right to work for a living, make your own way and not ask for handouts. If I didn't have the money and couldn't afford something, I didn't have it. I believe that this is a good and godly attitude, but it had created an area of pride in my life. On many occasions, my parents would ask if I needed money, and I had always told them that I didn't, because I didn't. I have to say that I took pride in the fact that I had never needed them to give me any financial help but that soon changed. Although I had finished building my house, and it was on the market to be sold, I still needed to pay the mortgage. I managed to live on the money I had saved, and the "God checks" that had come through the mail for almost a year. However, as time went on, I felt in my Spirit that it was right to accept the money my parents wanted to loan me. This was a new experience for me, as I had never borrowed money from any person. I swallowed my pride and accepted their help.

Again, I have to say that this was an amazing experience. The money was very helpful, but the gift of kindness was so much more. In their generosity, I was able to catch a glimpse of the love they had for me. Even though I felt that I had disappointed them and brought shame to the family, their concern and love for me was genuine. They were unable to travel to the States and throw their arms around me to reassure me in the way they wanted to. Even though they spent hours on the phone, encouraging me and offering words of hope, they were desperate to do more. Their words were not empty. They told me they loved me and demonstrated their love in every way they could, and one of those ways was sending money to help us. It's in times like these when we really appreciate family. The friends are in hiding, and people that hang onto your success in hope of getting a spot in the limelight are gone. My greatest friends, my family, were there, standing with me and helping us through this time.

As time went on, we overcame many financial mountains, but we were about to discover that the biggest one was before us. We still needed to sell the house that I had built. The house had a good amount of capital in it, half of which was Laura's. She had been patient but it was her money. I was also an Englishman, living in America and in order to work, I needed my green card. Obtaining this was months away.

By God's grace and provision all our bills were paid, and we didn't go without anything. Even though the house had been on the market for six months, no one had put in an offer. The housing market was quickly slowing down, but the house was on a great piece of land, finished with the highest quality, and there should have had plenty of interest. What was God doing? I don't believe that we should set our course in life and then run blindly into the future when something is obvious. It would have been easy to have kept receiving handouts and trusting God to continue to provide, but we felt God wanted to do something else.

Amanda and I decided that we would put it in God's hands and if we had not received any offer by the beginning of December, then we would enjoy Christmas together, after which I would return to the UK and work there so we could pay the bills until the house sold. It sounded like a wise decision; however it was painful for us. The decision was mixed with many questions such as "How long I would be gone? How long would we be apart? Would the house sell? How much would we get?" The deeper questions we had were, "Did God really want us to stay together given the mistakes we had made? Would God allow us to stay together or was this our punishment? Did God have a different outlook on the future that we didn't know about? How would we cope, how would the kids cope?"

Deep down, we believed that God had forgiven us and that we would stay together, but this belief would be tested in the next few weeks. As Christmas drew near, we did all we could for each other and the kids. We tried to stay positive and enjoy the season, but the knowledge that I might have to return to the UK was always in the back of our minds. December arrived and there had been no offers on the house. We had put this before God and made a decision. I would return to the UK just after New Year's Day. We had also decided that Amanda and the kids would move into the house until it sold. It wasn't wise to have two sets of bills and an empty house. So, Amanda moved in and I moved out! In our natural thinking, we thought the house would take at least three to six months to sell. Nothing really sells during the cold winter months in Maine, so we were waiting for spring.

Unless you have been in the position of leaving someone you love for an extended period of time, it's hard to imagine all the emotions we went through. People tried to understand where we were at and they encouraged us that it wouldn't be for a long. They told us that it would all turn out for good. There were others who were pleased that I was leaving the States, and they hoped that I would never return.

After having an amazing Christmas, saying good-bye was hard. Kissing the kids, telling them I loved them, and reassuring them I would be back soon, was difficult. We didn't know how long "soon" would be. Amanda and I left the house on a very cold winter's morning. Fresh snow was on the ground. Our bodies and hearts felt cold as we boarded the bus to Portland, Maine. In Portland, I would continue on to the Boston airport, and Amanda would return by bus to Bangor. All we could do as we traveled was hold each other, and reassure ourselves that God was in control, and all this would be behind us soon. We hoped the bus ride to Portland would be slow, but it went too fast. Once we arrived, we had a bit or time for breakfast before we had to say our good-byes.

The scene was all too familiar. The last time I was in this position, I was putting Laura on a plane and she was returning to England. She would never come back to the States. Again, I couldn't help but fear that this was a kind of payback, only this time, it was my turn to leave. Maybe God would never let me come back? Our good-bye was filled with hugs, tears and promises. As Amanda boarded her bus, our eyes remained fixed on each other until the bus pulled out of sight. In that moment, we both felt very lonely. Amanda had a two-hour journey back to Bangor with nothing more than her hopes and fears. I had another ten hours of traveling back to the UK where the unknown of my future was waiting for me.

When I finally arrived in England, in the early hours of the next morning, my Dad met me. He had a beaming smile on his face and his eyes danced with joy. He was so pleased to see me, and I was soon surrounded by the comfort of my parents' home. This was the home where I had grown up. It was familiar, friendly, warm and full of love. It was so good to be with them.

Even though I was home in England, and enjoyed being with my parents, my heart was three thousand miles away with Amanda and the kids. I called them at least twice a day. The first call would be to wake them up in the morning, and the second would be before they went to sleep that night. After a few days of adjustment and getting over jetlag, I set about the business of finding a job. The bills needed to be paid and I needed to take care of Amanda and the kids. After a great deal of praying and looking through the jobs in both the newspaper and on the Internet, I found what I thought would be a good opportunity. It was a job in marketing, and I liked the look of the challenge. I made the call, got an interview, and was offered the job. I would start the next day! All seemed to be good, but I just felt uneasy about it.

The next morning, before I started my new job, my sister Mandy took me for breakfast. We spent time talking about the past year and all that had happened. The pain, the repentance and also the hope I had in God. The conversation soon turned to my new job. As we were talking, I started to cry. I couldn't hold back the tears. I just felt it was wrong and I was doing something in my own strength, and that this was not part of God's plan. I knew it was right to be in England, but I was not sure about the job. The battle in my heart was that I wanted and needed to provide for Amanda and the kids, but I also knew that God had called me to the ministry and that this was not His plan.

Mandy, was encouraging and practical. She encouraged me to go to the job, and that I would know when I got there if I should be there or not. She also encouraged me, that if I didn't feel right about it, then I should leave. I took her advice and went to work. I was there for about thirty minutes. The conviction in my heart was overwhelming. I had to be obedient to the Lord, no matter how it looked to man. I informed the person training me, that this was not for me, and that I didn't want to waste anymore of his time. With that, I left, and to my parent's surprise, I was soon back at their home. I thank God that they are godly parents and that they understood my heart. It's important to be obedient to God, but being obedient isn't always easy; it can be painful to trust. I still had bills to pay, and there had been no interest in the house. Worst of all, I still had no idea when I would see Amanda and the kids again.

There was nothing else to do but set the next day for prayer and fasting. I believe there is an increase in God's power when we make the sacrifice to fast. When we deny ourselves our natural desires to discover God's will, He honors that sacrifice and speaks into our lives. It was the 10th of January, and I needed to hear from God. I needed to know that God to heard my prayers. This would be a day of learning for me. I had no problem in praying and having confidence that God would hear and answer my prayers. But, according to the Bible, that confidence only comes when we pray for the will of God.

> Now this is the confidence that we have in Him, that if we ask anything according to His will, He hears us. And if we know that He hears us, whatever we ask, we know that we have the petitions that we have asked of Him (1 John 5:14-15)

I had to discover what the will of God was. Did He want me to be with Amanda or not? Was it His will to sell the house or just mine? I had to face my fears and lay down my own desire before God. I asked Him to show me what He wanted, and I confessed that I was willing to do whatever He wanted me to do for the sake of the kingdom. When we get to the place of surrender, every prayer is scary because we are not sure what God will ask of us. I also believe that God looks at our heart, and He knows if we are genuine in our surrender, or if it's just words. I believe that God wanted me to die to myself, and my own desires before I could move forward. I don't believe that I could have come to this place in my heart if I was still in the States, as my mind and heart was full of emotions. I had to be separate, yet in a safe environment. I needed to be willing and desperate for God to speak.

The first thing God said was not an answer to my prayers, but a question. He asked if I was willing to lay my life down for Amanda and the children. Would I be willing to live in Bangor for a time, should that be His will? This was difficult for me, as I always had the willingness to go anywhere He wanted. I had a desire to travel the world and if God should call me to stay in one place longer than I had desired, it would be hard. To make matters worse, I really didn't want to live in Bangor because everybody new my past and the mistakes I had made. It also meant that if I went back to the States in the near future, I would not be able to work for a time, as I needed my green card. I would have to put the ministry on hold.

God had backed me into a corner. I shared in an earlier chapter that we need to put God first, then family and then the ministry. I had not always gotten this formula right. I had often put the ministry before family, working many hours a week. It was a time to choose the right thing, and so I committed to doing whatever God wanted. He would be first in my life, but I chose to put my family before the ministry. Let me clarify this point. I was not choosing the family instead of the ministry, but I was choosing not to neglect their needs while doing the work of the ministry. With this act of surrender, I felt and knew God's heart. In a moment, He filled my heart with answers. The overwhelming thing that came into my heart was that God had forgiven me for past mistakes and that He was releasing me to remain with Amanda and make her my wife. I was so relieved that God hadn't called me to live the rest of my life celibate.

All I could think of was King David, and all that had happened between him and Bathsheba. David had made some terrible mistakes. However, when he came to himself, he truly repented. God didn't tell him to leave Bathsheba and move on with his life. David now had a responsibility to take care of her, and to abandon her would have been another mistake. The grace of God is that Bathsheba eventually gave birth to Solomon. Solomon was the son who would be king after David's death, and be known as the wisest man in the entire world. That's mind blowing! A WOW kind of grace! Some might question this, and wonder why God didn't tell me to go back to Laura. Since our divorce, Laura had also moved on with her life, and was seeing someone else. It wasn't a time to look back, but forward.

Once I came to the place of knowing the heart of God, I had great faith to pray for more manna from heaven. I knew the housing market in the States was in a slump, and that it was not a good time of year to sell. This made it an ideal season for God to show His grace and His power! Both Amanda and I also knew that there were some people who were speaking "doom and gloom," saying they never thought the house would sell, and that I would not return to the States. Once I knew it was God's will for me to be with Amanda, I was able to set my face and pray earnestly for the house to sell. The next morning, I woke to a day of miracles. God is faithful. When we position ourselves in the place that God wants us, He can start to move in a greater measure in our lives. From a place of surrender came God's supply.

When I called Amanda that morning, she told me that the estate agency had called her and that there was someone that wanted to see the house. They had been by once before but no offer had been made and there was no sale in sight. By that evening, the interested couple who turned out to be Christians made an offer. The offer was below what I wanted, but I was desperate for a sale. I trusted God and asked what I should do. I believe God told me to refuse the first offer, so I did. I then waited, wondering if I had really heard God and made the right decision. After a few hours, which felt like years of silence, the second offer came. I refused again, and finally, after a much shorter time, a third offer was made.

It was at this point that I felt God put a figure in my heart and I decided to tell them what I was willing to accept. To everyone's great delight they accepted my request and made their offer. This came via the Internet at exactly 11pm (the time in England) on January 11th. The house was sold!

Was it a coincidence that I had come to a place of surrender the day before? Even more astonishing was that the sale of the house had been agreed upon on the 11th January at 11pm. For some time Amanda and I had talked about the "eleventh hour God" and how He always turns up and meets the need at the last minute. We thought the eleventh hour was December 1st, God had another plan, and He *"opened the windows of heaven and poured down a blessing that we could not contain". (Malachi 3:10)* It was manna from heaven. In the midst of the wilderness, God had proven that He was unchanging and faithful. Even though we had messed up, He was still the provider and He loved His kids. God blew us away with His grace!

With the sale of the house final, the fear of the unknown behind us, and with a bit of money to burn, a flight was booked for Amanda. She joined me the next week and together we enjoyed being with my family before returning to the States together. In the days before Amanda arrived, I thought God was finished teaching me the lessons He wanted me to learn while I was in England. I was mistaken. There was a lot more to discover.

Chapter 8
RESTORING THE DREAM

A person without dreams or desires for the future is usually a very sad individual, with little self-worth or belief in themselves. A person who has a dream, looks to the future with hope. No matter what they may be going through in their life, they have the ability to see beyond the challenges, into the future promises.

I have always been a person who has been able to dream. I have found it easy to catch a glimpse of what the future might look like, and am able to run after it and make it happen. I love talking to people and discovering the gifts they have, or dreams that have hidden in their hearts. It's a joy to be able to encourage people to chase after the things that God has called them to. I believe it's the responsibility of those who have been called into ministry, to help discover the gift that others have, and enable them to cultivate it. (Ephesians 4:11)

I am not ashamed to declare that I am a dreamer! The problem arises when I stop dreaming or start believing that I am unworthy to do the things I once dreamed about. When we see things that were once just a thought, or impression that God put on our hearts, take form and become real, is amazing. However, when through our own choices, we watch those visions crumble, we become a broken people with broken dreams.

Before I made my trip to England, I had come to a place where I was transitioning from a "sinning saint" to a "repentant saint". I was experiencing the love of God and understanding His forgiveness for my sins. This in itself brought a restored joy in my heart, as I knew I had set things right with God. I was walking in relationship with Him. Yet, through all this, I still carried sadness in my heart because I knew the things that I had been called of God to do. No matter how much I had encouraged others in the past, telling those who had fallen and made mistakes, that God was not finished with them, and that their best years were still ahead, I had trouble believing this for myself. What did I have to offer? I had many accomplishments in the ministry in the past, but I had also messed up big time. Who would listen to me? Who would want to? The biggest question of all was, "Would God still anoint me to do the things He had called me to do?" No matter how gifted I was, without the anointing and the power of the Holy Spirit, I would have little impact in the lives of others. My ability to help others change and grow would be limited, because without Him, I was nothing.

The other problem was that I didn't want to be like the athlete that goes into retirement, and when he comes out of retirement for another run, and fails to make the grade. The sport critics are quick to declare "He or she are past their best," or, "They were great once." How many times have we heard similar statements in the church, referring to ministers who have gone through hard times? People are quick to declare, "They were anointed once," or "They're just not the same." For me, there must be another problem other than the anointing. Perhaps it is due to lack of self-worth, or confidence, lethargy, or the lost desire to deliver a message. If you're anointed, you are anointed. In addition, if God restores He does a perfect job, and fully restores. *(Galatians 6:1)*

There were family members and ministers that encouraged me and told me that God still wanted to use me, and that He had a plan and purpose for my life. Their words were helpful, but I needed to hear it from God. He had called me the first time, and should He want to use me again, I needed to hear His voice again.

I felt in my heart that God was not finished with me. Everyday I thought about the ministry. It's difficult to run from what God calls you to. When I returned to England, I found myself in familiar and secure surroundings. This was also the place that I had heard the call of God the first time. I was sleeping in my parents home, a place where we had seen many people worshiping God, being healed and accepting Jesus as Lord. My Christian experience had started there. There were the friends around me who I had known for years, all of which had made decisions for Jesus around the same time that I had. As we talked, our conversation was Christ-centered and we often wondered what was next for me. When was I going to minister again? How did I see the future unfolding?

My family also surrounded me. I had the privilege of leading them all to Jesus at different times. I had employed my brother as youth pastor, and he had worked alongside me in ministry for ten years. They had heard my messages, and now they were waiting to see what I would do. Would I follow what I had preached? Would I stop feeling sorry for myself and instead, get up and do the things God had called me to? Or would I wallow in self-pity and accept defeat?

The more time I spent in England, the more I prayed about the future and the call of God. Everywhere I went there was a memory of what God had done through my life and how He had called me. I started to feel a familiar tug on the heart as desire was returning. I knew what I was called to do, and with great desire, I wanted to do it. I could only ask, "God, will you anoint me again? Will you fully restore me and use me according to your purposes?" During those four weeks in England, God spoke to me through many people, as they encouraged me about the future. But most importantly, I started to hear God speak to me again, reaffirming the things He had put in my heart.

The dreams and visions that had been distorted, began to come back into focus, taking shape in my heart. One night while I was in my parent's home, after everyone had gone to bed, I was praying and I clearly heard God say, "This was one of the reasons I brought you back to England." He wanted to remind me of His promises and hear His call to the ministry again. He told me that everything had a purpose, even the job I had gone for and walked away from.

My response was simple, "Ok Jesus, if this is true, show it to me in your Word." God instantly led me to read about Peter, and I started to see things that were important to Peter's restoration, and mine.

Peter was always at the forefront of what was happening in Jesus' ministry. He wanted to have a go at everything. His passion and desire for Jesus created a zeal that propelled him a little bit further than most of the other disciples. He wasn't satisfied with sitting in a boat. He too wanted to walk on water, with Jesus. He desired to be more holy in his pursuit of the Kingdom, to the point that he thought he would go one better than everyone else, by declaring that he didn't just want his feet washed, but his hands and his head also! *(John 13:8)* He got top marks in the test when Jesus asked the disciples *"Who do the people say that I am?"* While some said he was a prophet, Peter said, *"You are the Christ"* (John 13:16) Well done, Peter! He got it right! He was on a spiritual high. Everyone could see his wisdom, and then he put his foot in his mouth. He said to Jesus "I will never stumble (or deny you)." You can sense the moment, he said it, that his fall was just around the corner.

We know what happens. Jesus proclaims that Peter would deny him three times, and as we know, Peter fulfills the prophetic word. We find him fallen from his position of greatness. He has made a mistake, a big mistake. How could he spend three years with Jesus, seeing all the miracles, and still come to a place where he could betray his friend by denying Him. Is this not the worst thing a person could do? *(Luke 22:31-34, John 18:15-18)*

The first thing we have to understand is, that whenever we sin, and for whatever reason we sin, we are denying Christ as Lord. Jesus is only Lord when we are obedient. When we choose to disobey Him and do what we want, we become lord of our own lives, and take over the throne in our hearts. The action could be as simple as gossiping. God has told us gossip is a sin just like adultery. We could easily produce a list of sins. However, sin is sin. The self-imposed consequences will differ depending on what we have done, but sin is still sin. If we murder someone, we go to prison. You won't go to prison for gossiping, but you are still destroying a life!

Understanding the way God sees sin and His forgiveness, is the start of restoration. The question for Peter was, "Is he now no longer one of the so called, elite?" He was called to lead the newly formed church. *(Matthew 16:18)* Would he still be able to fulfill his potential after such a mistake? The good news is, our future is not dependent on what people think or the judgments they make, it is dependent on the grace of God, and how He chooses to use us. God started to speak to me about Peter's sin and restoration. I was able to see comparisons in my own life. My sin was different, but the God who restores is always the same.

> *"But go tell His disciples – and Peter that He is going before you to Galilee, there you will see Him as He said to you" (Mark 16:7)*

This is a remarkable passage. Mary Magdalene goes to the tomb to find Jesus after His crucifixion. Jesus is not there, and she meets an angel who instructs her to gather the disciples, "and Peter" together. Why was there this special instruction about Peter? Was it because the other disciples were struggling with what Peter had done, or was it that Peter was struggling? I think it was both. Peter and the disciples needed to be reminded that Peter had been called of God, and that he was not to be forgotten at this time. This is a wonderful insight into how God accepts us even after we have messed up. Then, we read the remarkable account in the book of John of how Jesus met Peter.

> *After these things Jesus showed himself again to the disciples at the sea of Tiberias, and in this manner He showed himself: Simon Peter, Thomas called the twin, Nathanael of Cana in Galilee, the sons of Zebedee and two others of His disciples were together. Simon Peter said to them, "I am going fishing." They said to him, "we are going with you also." They went out and immediately got into the boat,*

and that night they caught nothing. But when the morning had now come, Jesus stood on the shore; yet the disciples did not know that it was Jesus. Then Jesus said to them, "Children have you any food?" they answered Him "no." And He said to them, "cast the net on the right side of the boat, and you will find some." So they cast and now they were not able to draw it in because of the multitude of fish. Therefore the disciple whom Jesus loved said to Peter, "It is the Lord!" Now when Simon Peter heard that it was the Lord, he put on his outer garment (for he had removed it) and plunged into the sea. (John 21:1-8)

All this takes place just before the disciples have breakfast on the beach with Jesus, and before Jesus questions Peter about how much he loves Him, resulting in Him restoring Peter to ministry. The process that takes place before Jesus reaffirms Peter's call to the ministry is remarkable. The first thing we see is that Peter goes back to his safe place. He attempts to go fishing. He has no idea of what the future holds, so he does that which he knows he is good at. If he could catch fish before and make a living, he can do it again. What did he have to lose? The disciples go through a whole night trying to catch fish.

When we try to do things in our own strength, or run from what we should be doing, it's a long, drawn out, dark process. If we call this process a night season, we have a better understanding of how the disciples felt after fishing all night. The good news is, that when morning came, Jesus was waiting to speak to them, just as He is waiting to speak to us.

Then He got into one of the boats which was Simon's (Peter) and asked him to put out a little from land. And He sat down and taught the multitudes from the boat. When He had stopped speaking, He said to Simon, "launch out into the deep and let down your nets for a catch." But Simon answered and said to Him, "Master we have toiled all night and caught nothing; nevertheless at your word I will let down the net" And when they had done this, they caught a great number of fish and their net was breaking:.......... So when they had brought their boats to land they forsook all and followed Him (Luke 5: 3-6 & 11)

Matthew 4:18 tells us that Jesus called them to follow Him, and *"he would make them fishers of men."* I do not think it's a coincidence that Jesus meets Peter at the ocean to reaffirm his calling. I can only imagine that when Jesus called out to Peter from the beach, after they had caught a multitude of fish, that Peter was reminded of his first encounter with Jesus, His calling, and the three years of ministry that followed. I believe God brought him to a familiar place with an intention of reminding him of all He had called him from and all He had called him to.

I know that when I went to England, I returned to what I knew I could do. I tried to get a secular job, but God did not allow it. Instead, He reminded me of every place I had ministered in, and every time He had spoken to me regarding my calling. This was the start of ministerial restoration. God brings us to a place, where He reaffirms His love and calling. In the midst of people's judgmental attitudes, and our own self-doubt and pity party, God speaks. Not only do we hear His voice, we understand His heart. He is our Father who sees a brighter future for His children. We have received the "telling off", a knowing that it's time again for instruction, empowering, encouraging and releasing.

Getting back to how Jesus restored Peter, we see that Jesus brought him to a place of remembrance by meeting him at the ocean, and directing him where to throw the net. When they were reunited, they all ate breakfast, enjoying fellowship together. This was a great response to the emotional highs and lows that had taken place over the past few days. They all had to deal with Jesus being crucified, the resurrection, Judas' betrayal, and Peter walking out. Their feelings must have been at fever pitch. They were trying to keep it together, and not say the wrong thing, but they were probably still wondering about Peter stability. What was he thinking and what did the future hold?

Jesus created an opportunity to have some fun. I am sure they laughed together, talked about the past three years of ministry, and then it was time to address the problem. What would happen with Peter? Jesus asked him, *"Do you love me?"* Imagine the silence as everyone stopped talking and eating, and they tuned their ears to the conversation. Think about what happens in present time if you fall while being in ministry. People start questioning, what will happen. We wonder what God is saying in the mist of another minister messing up? We question the effects of the mistakes and whether the individual will be able to overcome them, and if so, what does their future look like?

Some of these issues depend on a man's ability to repent, forgive themselves, and courage to pick up the baton again to start running towards the goal. Yes, it takes courage! Everyone is pointing the finger and watching, wondering if you will make it, and questioning whether you will fall again. No matter how forgiven we are, some people that have fallen don't have the stomach, or courage, to get back up. This leaves the church thinking that God refused to fully restore the person who had sinned. This gives us a warped view of God's grace.

When we look at Jesus talking with Peter, we see God's desire for full restoration. Jesus asked Peter three times how much he loved Him. Jesus didn't point out the mistake Peter made, He didn't need to. Peter was fully aware of his mistake, and was carrying the guilt that came with it. Jesus didn't give Peter the chance to wallow in his fall or to have a pity party. The mistake was in the past. Now the question in the heart of God is, how to move forward and get on with the job of the great commission?

"Peter, do you love me?" When we think about love, it encompasses so many thoughts and actions. It speaks of relationship, sacrifice, serving, laying down our own lives for another, working as a team

and putting others first. Jesus didn't focus on the mistake Peter made, but on the condition of his heart. Jesus could have said, "Do you have what it takes to drag yourself out of self-condemnation, making a go of this thing we started?" Many of us will fall but our restoration really depends on how we respond to God. Do we still love Him? Do we still want to put Him first and serve Him? When we get to the place of saying yes to these questions, as with Peter, we hear His voice, *"Feed my lambs."* When we realize we still love Him and want the things of the kingdom, we stop hearing our own voice that says we can't, and we begin to hear His command to go!! Each time Jesus asked Peter about his love, Peter responded positively, and Jesus re-affirmed His commission – *"Feed my lambs, tend my sheep, feed my sheep"* Jesus restores the vision in his heart so he could dream again. Not only were these words of encouragement to Peter, but the other disciples also heard them. The disciples were able to catch hold of the heart of Jesus, and encourage Peter in the calling. They were not left wondering about Peter's future, but were given the opportunity to help empower him.

It was in this encouraging environment, that Jesus dealt with the attitude that had led to Peter's mistake. Just because we have repented, doesn't always mean we have changed our bad attitudes. They need to be addressed and changed, if we are to have a successful future.

> *"Most assuredly, I say to you, when you were younger, you girded yourself and walked where you wished; but when you are old you will stretch out your hands and another will gird you and carry you where you do not wish" (John 21:18)*

This scripture speaks prophetically about Peter's future. It revealed how he would die at the hands of persecutors. The man that once denied Christ, would in the end, stand victoriously in his confession of Christ and be martyred as a result. I firmly believe that if we have fallen into an area of sin, we will face the same challenge again in the future. Our prayer is that we have corrected the character flaws that led to our initial destruction, and when faced with the same temptation, we will be victorious. When we look at this scripture in its context, we see that Jesus reaffirmed Peter's calling. He assured him that he would still be used to bring the kingdom of God. However, it was time for him to grow up, and stop living life the way he wanted to. It was time to be wise, and allow God to lead him, as he ministered to others.

God wants to bring full restoration, but to do so, adjustments need to be made. When I was going through this process in England, God made me very aware that He was not finished with me. He still had a plan for my life. However, during this time, He revealed areas in my life where I had been unwise, and done things the way I wanted to. God doesn't want us to make the same mistake twice, so we have to change the attitude that led to the mistakes, making adjustments before He will release us back into ministry. Once Jesus had caught hold of Peters' heart, and brought him to a place of confessing his love, He dealt with Peter's attitudes. Then, He spoke the same words He had used to call him the first time, *"Follow me"* (Matthew 4:19, John 21:19)

In times of restoration, God doesn't always give us new words or prophecies. Rather, He reminds us of the ones we received in the past. His word is the same; He doesn't need to say it again in a different way because our calling hasn't changed. We have to take hold of what God has said, and by faith, start stepping out. God had spoken to me many times through scripture and prophetic words. It was time for me to stand on His words and do what He wanted me to do. One of the things we have to deal with in being restored into ministry is areas of insecurity. I can honestly say that throughout my years in ministry, I have never been insecure. We learn to do the things God tells us to do and we do them confidently. Confidence in God and the things He calls us to, gives us the ability to encourage and empower others.

The pulpit in the church becomes a platform not only for our own ministry, but also for those in the congregation. It's easy to invite a guest speaker because no matter how good or bad they are, they leave after the service. However, the heart of God for those in ministry is to, *"Equip the saints for the work of the ministry,"* *(Ephesians 4:12).* We must start this equipping process in our own churches. The challenge is that some people prefer the style and delivery of those you are training to yours. Ministers have to come to terms with the fact that we are all different, and God anoints us in different ways. Our gift will touch and inspire different people at different times. When we understand this we can deal with our insecurities.

The biggest challenge comes when we have made mistakes. Our confidence is low and we wonder if we will be anointed in the same way or if we will operate at a lower lever of ministry. I believe Peter struggled with this very thing:

> *Then Peter, turned around, saw the disciple whom Jesus loved, following, who also had leaned on His breast at the supper, and said, "Lord, who is the one who betrays you?" Peter seeing Him, said to Jesus "But Lord, what about this man?" Jesus said to him, "If I will that he remain till I come, what is that to you? You follow me?"* *(John 21:20-23)*

Peter's insecurity was revealed when he "turned around". He stopped looking at Jesus, and placed His eyes on a man (John). In a moment, his perspective changed from a godly outlook on the future, to an earthly perspective of rating himself alongside a fellow minister. It seems from scripture that Peter and John were closer to Jesus than the other disciples. Peter witnessed John's closeness to Him at the last supper. It's my belief, that Peter, who had felt like an equal to John, prior to his denial of Christ, now felt "second best, causing him to question Jesus about John.

When we have fallen or made mistakes, it's easy to look at others and question whether we are still equal, or if we have slipped to second best. The response to Peter is good for us to hear. Jesus said, *"What is it to you?"* Why do we concern ourselves about what God is going to do with others? When we are first called into the ministry, and we see God working in our lives, we grow in confidence in God using us for His work. When we fall, we see our weakness. In the process of restoration, we look at our peers through our weaknesses and not our strengths. It is in these moments, that we need a godly perspective. It's God *"who chooses the weak things in this world to confuse the wise." (1 Corinthians 1:27)* We don't get any weaker than a person who has messed up! Instead of looking at those around us and making comparisons, we need to understand that God has called us, and He will use us to the measure of His grace. *(Ephesians 4:7)*

What I find encouraging about Peter is, that he became a better minister after his fall. Jesus declared that He would *"build his church on the Rock,"* which was the name He gave to Peter *(Matthew 16:18)*. After Peter fell, he was restored into ministry and led the newly formed church in Jerusalem where he did greater works for many years.

Just because we have made mistakes, we don't have to view it as the end or the decline of our ministry. The result depends on our attitude, and how we choose to believe God for the future. I believe that God can take our mistakes and turn them around for His Kingdom. If we choose to be honest and open with our past it can be the start of a better future.

This was a great time in Peter's life. Jesus reaffirmed him time and again in regards to the ministry to which he had been called. My trip to England turned out to be an amazing time of growth and insight, as I opened my heart and heard the call of God again. However, we have to go from hearing what God tells us to action. Are we willing to take a step of faith and walk into what God has called us to? Yes, there will be opposition, but there will also be great favor. We see in the life of Peter that he took this step of faith and started using his gift:

And in those days Peter stood up in the midst of the disciples (altogether the number of names was about a hundred and twenty) and said (Acts 1:15)

But Peter standing up with the eleven, raised his voice and said to them, "Men of Judea and all who dwell in Jerusalem, let this be know to you and heed my words" (Acts 2:14)

Peter *"stood up"* and spoke in these two accounts. He first stood up in the midst of the disciples, and then the disciples joined him and stood up to the world. To stand up after you have fallen takes courage and faith to act on what God has told you to do. People will question our calling, and wonder if we have the right to minister, but we have to choose to believe God and act on it.

The first group Peter rose up and spoke to were his friends and fellow ministers. This was a behind close doors meeting! He spoke to those who knew him well, and those who would encourage him. Some of them were with him when Jesus reassured him of his calling. Once he ministered to them, he was released again under the anointing of the Holy Spirit to minister in the open and to the world. This was a significant part of his restoration. With restoration, there has to be a place and time that we begin to minister again. Usually we first minister to those who know us and who are familiar with what we have come through. Once we have been faithful in this area, God will start opening more doors for us to minister to the larger church.

It is this same process, that God brought me through. When I left England and returned to the United States, it felt like a new beginning. Amanda and I were excited because we knew that God was with us, and that He had a plan for our lives. We could look towards the future and start to dream. With this in mind, we had to start taking steps of faith and taking action towards what God had spoken to us. This was a small beginning, but as we were faithful in little, God opened more doors.

The first opportunity to minister came for me in a morning Bible study. For a time before I went to England, I had been going to a Bible study that met at the local trendy café' with a group of men. It was informal meeting to discuss challenges we had or what we had discovered about God that week. Even though I had been going for a while, I was reluctant to share a great deal. It wasn't my ministry or Bible study, I just went to get out of the house and be encouraged. The first time I met with the group after I returned from England, I found that I had a new desire to share Biblical truth and when the opportunity came, I shared a bit about what I felt the scriptures were saying. The group was encouraged and Paul, the minister, asked me to keep going with the subject I had brought up. The other men were open and hungry for more, drawing out my gift to teach. I left that day feeling I had helped someone and the desire to minister increased.

The following week, at the same Bible study, the minister was unable to attend. The same men turned up and no one else had much to share. Then, one of the men asked about his gift and what he should do with it. I started to encourage the group to use the gifts that God had given them to help the church grow. I also encouraged them to submit themselves to ministry and do all they could do to support the church they were in. The conversation took off and other people joined in. This was another step in God's restoration.

The reason for sharing this second encounter of a "behind closed doors ministry," is because it gave me an opportunity to encourage people in supporting the church we were going to. When we are going through restoration, it is easy to be tempted to promote ourselves in an effort to try and find some self worth. We can fall into the trap of talking about our past accomplishments to "woo" people into listening to what we are saying, and to get their approval. Some people also see this kind of environment as an opportunity to lay a foundation for their own ministry in the future. This is a very dangerous attitude.

I believe that there is a time in restoration that we get to minister in the church we are attending. It is imperative that we show respect and submit to the minister of that church. No matter who is "more gifted" or more experienced, we are able to attend that church due to the grace they have shown us. It is right to show respect and support for the leadership of the church we are attending. The more we support them, the more they will trust us to minister to the congregation. We have to understand that the moment a minister takes on the process of restoring another minister, they become open to attack from those who are judgmental from outside the church. There are people in the church, who watch what the minister does with us. When they give us an opportunity to minister, they are risking ridicule and possibly losing people in the congregation. Our response to their grace should always be respectful and supportive.

The next stage in restoring the gift, took me by surprise. Amanda, the children and I had been going to church regularly. Most of the congregation knew who we were and our backgrounds, but there were also a few people that did not know our history. While we were in church, our only aim was to worship God with all that we had and to be an example in worship to others. We had no intent to minister into people's lives. Our ministry was to God as worshipers. During one service, as I was worshiping God, I heard the Holy Spirit speak to me, giving me a prophetic word for the church. I knew it was God, but I wrestled with sharing it in the church. I was nervous about how I would be received. I was also aware, that if I stood up to share, Pastor Paul would be faced with questions after the service. I decided not to share the things God put in my heart. When we left church that day, I put it out of my mind and forgot about it.

The following week, we attended church as always and started to worship God. Instantly, the same word filled my heart, and this time with greater revelation. I was faced with the same challenge of whether I should speak or not. I quickly mumbled a prayer under my breath that I hoped God didn't really hear. "Lord if you want me to share this word, then lead Pastor Paul into a time of allowing the church to use the gift of prophecy." I had barely finished praying, when Paul encouraged the church to share the things God had laid on their hearts. In that moment, I heard many messages that I had preached to others in my own head, encouraging them to use the gifts that God had given them. "Step out in faith, don't miss the moment!" With great hesitation, I approached Paul, and shared with him the things God had put in my heart. I didn't want to overstep the authority God had placed in the church, and I knew that he would have to deal with any repercussions. I laid the gifts and the word at his feet.

As Paul listened to the word, he encouraged me to share it with the church. Even though I was nervous, as soon as I opened my mouth, God filled my heart with boldness. The gift flowed out of me and people began to be touched by the Word. It was clear that God was using this word, at this time, to open hearts and to minister to people. Once I had finished, Pastor Paul took up the things that God had spoken to me, and started to encourage the church in a similar way. The prophetic word with Paul's encouragement, opened up a dynamic encounter in the church that day, and gave room for the Holy Spirit to move and touch lives. God was using me again, but I would have to be patient for the next opportunity.

As we continued to attend the church, we felt it was necessary not to do minimum service, but to become more connected. We decided that we needed to commit to more than a Sunday service, and started attending the midweek service along with other events offered by the church. As we took this step of faith, God started to open more doors to use us to encourage other people in the church. The Wednesday evening service became a great outlet for us in ministering to others. It was a time when the church was less structured and more open to the gifts that God had given people. Pastor Paul had a heart to see other people used, and he encouraged everyone to be used of God.

During one of these Wednesday evening services, the church was ministering to the Lord in praise and worship. There was a real sense that God was going to do something different. The normal songs and pattern of worship was abandoned as the Holy Spirit led and moved the worship leaders in times of inspiration and prophetic singing. As the music died down, and we were waiting to see what else God would do, Pastor Paul shared a word that God had just put in his Spirit about bringing our hearts to the altar.

I had been studying that week about the altar David spoke about in the Old Testament. As Paul was speaking, the revelation I had received earlier in the week was flooding my heart. The next moment, Paul looked at me, and said, "the Holy Spirit has just told me that you have an understanding about altars that we need to hear". Again, he gave me a platform to minister to others. The things God had put in my heart flowed out of my mouth and ministered to the church. After the service, many people came and told me how much they had received during the time I had ministered. No matter how much I gave in revelation that day, opening people to receive from God, I received much more in encouragement. The dream God had put in my heart for the future was growing, and none of it was through my own efforts to push myself forward. God was in control, and He was leading the way for our restoration.

As I have shared in previous chapters, I have a great desire to see the Holy Spirit move and minister in the lives of the church. He is the one who brings refreshing and strength to the weary. It's the Holy Spirit that empowers a person to make the changes they need to make in their lives, or to do the things that God requires of them. Sharing the Word in a meeting is one thing, but we need the ministry of the Holy Spirit to implant it into the hearts of the congregation, moving them in a way that brings about genuine change. I was in a place where I knew God was able to use me in the word, but would He also use me to release the anointing of the Holy Spirit to others.

After Jesus was baptized and began His ministry, He told the people that His ability to preach, heal the sick, release those who were bound and bring freedom to lives was through the Spirit of God and the anointing. *(Luke 4:18)* If Jesus needed the anointing of the Holy Spirit to minister, successfully, so do we. When we look at the New Testament church in the Book of Acts, we see great signs and wonders that are often attributed to the anointing of the Holy Spirit I like what Peter said when ministering to the man at the gates called Beautiful:

> *"Then Peter said, "Silver and Gold I do not have but what I have I give to you: In the name of Jesus of Nazareth, rise up and walk" (Acts 3:6)*

Peter had a power from God to heal the sick and he gave it away. He released the gift and the anointing that God had placed in his life and the man was healed. I know that God had used me to see the sick healed and people ministered to through the power of the Holy Spirit. If I wanted to give it away I had to make sure I had it!!

With a passion burning in my heart to see people ministered to, I set myself to prayer and called on God to anoint me, and use me to release His power to others again. I would stand in the living room or go into my bedroom and call on God, and then wait until I felt His presence. The more I felt Him, the more I asked for increase. It was there, in the secret place, that God filled me time and again with His presence. I knew if I could get it, I could give it away. I was being filled to overflowing with the power of the Holy Spirit.

It was after this time of receiving, that I attended another Wednesday night service. Again, the worship went off the map and started flowing where the Holy Spirit led. The Lord put a word in my heart in regards to bitterness and how it stops people. I asked permission to share what God had placed in my heart, and I was given the freedom to minister. Once I had finished sharing the word, I encouraged people to allow the Spirit of God to start operating in their hearts, allowing Him to minister to them. It was at this point, that I thought my part in the service was done. As I was about to go back to my seat, Pastor Paul asked me to minister to a couple. One couple led to another couple, and before long, there were many people being touched and filled with the Holy Spirit. God was using me to bring a release of His anointing and lives were being transformed.

When we minister in the Holy Spirit, we listen to voice of God, allowing us to minister prophetic words to people, or open a person's heart with words of knowledge. There is so much to be said about this subject of ministry, but the key is to listen to the Holy Spirit, and be obedient. Jesus ministered in many different ways, using different methods. What is good and timely for one person may not be what's required for another. Our hearts' desire needs to be to minister under the anointing of the Holy Spirit. When we are obedient to His voice, we speak what God has spoken, bringing encouraging words of freedom and hope.

When I ministered to people in the church during Wednesday night services, I had spoken small words of prophecy and encouragement, but not to a level that I was satisfied with. I had experienced much more in the past, and I believe in full restoration. My expectation was that God was going to increase this gift again.

The breakthrough came during a men's retreat weekend. The men were standing together, allowing the Holy Spirit to minister. As I looked around, the Holy Spirit dropped things into my heart about every person. I could have started a prophetic service, but I didn't feel a release to do that. It was enough for me to experience that God was opening my heart and the gift again in my life.

There had been times in the past when I would minister, I could look at a person, and God would fill my heart with revelation, a prophecy, or a word that would release that person. That gift was being stirred up in me again. During the weekend, God released me to speak a prophetic word into the life of one of the men. I shared the word given to me and went back to my place. Once ministry was done, the individual expressed that the prophetic word was accurate, and that I had "read his mail". God was restoring the gifts He had placed in my life.

The restoration of my ministry was similar to Peter's in that his opportunities to minister started with those he knew in a smaller, private setting, before it was released on a more public level. God starts restoration in a safe environment and then He releases us in a greater way. It is a progression, not an overnight event. God has to lay a new foundation and reignite the gifts in our lives. With me, every opportunity to minister brought a new release of something God had used me for in my past. Another key element of restoration is that it starts in an environment of submission. If we are not willing to lay our life down for others, God cannot lift it up to help others. Once we laid our hearts and lives down, and submitted to the ministry of Word of Life church, God started to open other doors. It was during the latter part of this process of restoration that ministers started calling and invited me to preach in their churches.

The first church we ministered in was very exciting because Amanda and I got to minister together. During our time of submission, God was speaking and molding both of us into the ministers He wanted us to be. As we talked and dreamed together about the future, we were certain of one thing —that God wanted us to be a team and minister together. It was awesome to preach that day, but my real joy was seeing Amanda praying for people, and having insight as she ministered to others. When we compared our experiences after the service, we discovered that God was saying the same things to us about the same people. God had made us one flesh and this was the start of greater things. That first church experience led to other church experiences where we ministered together and many people were touched.

A year after my return from England, many things had changed. It was obvious that God was leading us and His favor was on our lives. Amanda and I got married, and I felt like I was the most blessed man in the world. Not only was God giving me a second chance, He had given me a wonderful wife who desired the things of God as I did. We had more than a hope for the future, we had the promises of God, which are a sure foundation.

My Green Card was granted by U.S Government, which released me to work. It was at this time that God led me to start a Church Consultancy Business or ministry called "Cre8 Consultancy". I believe this was God's way of connecting me with other churches and ministers again while providing an income. Amanda and I were now married, and I was able to work and minister. God continued to open doors for us to preach. It wasn't long before we were being asked to consider taking on a church that had been without a pastor for a couple of years. Amanda and I joined the church in prayer to guide us into what God wanted. It seemed like a great opportunity, and part of God's plan in being fully restored.

With this opportunity before us, Amanda and I visited the United Kingdom (UK) to spend the New Year with my family. We had a wonderful time. The pain and suffering that we were going through the year before had gone, and there was joy in our hearts. Everyone was happy and we were able to fully enjoy the time we had. While in the UK, Amanda and I went to the church I had started, some thirteen years earlier. The people received us with great love, and our hearts were moved with joy and acceptance. It was during this service, that God started to stir my heart again with all the promises that He had made and the things He had called me to do in regards to church planting and networking. What was God doing?

We returned to the States, still unsure if we should pursue the pastoral position in the church we had ministered at a number of times, or if God had something else in mind. Again, we set ourselves to pray, and I asked Amanda if she would be willing to do anything and go anywhere for God. She responded with a positive, yes! Then she asked me, if I would be willing to stay in Bangor and start a new church. My head screamed, NO! However, I knew if this was God's will, then I would be more than willing. After we prayed, Amanda went to work, but the words she spoke kept coming back into my heart. In fact, they bugged me all day. By the day's end, I had submitted myself in a real way, and told God I was willing to start a church in Bangor if He gave us a worship leader.

The next morning I received a call from a worship leader who had been ministering for thirty years. He told me that God had spoken to him and that he believed God was calling him to be part of the church I was going to start! "Ok, God, if this is you, do something in my heart!" It was in that moment, that God reminded me that Peter had been restored to an apostolic ministry. God had called me to an apostolic ministry years ago. Even though I believed God would bring restoration, I had always wondered if He would restore the apostolic calling. God spoke to me again, and said that as He restored Peter, so He was restoring me to the apostolic ministry. I accepted that, but I asked, "Now what does that mean?" Instantly, I heard the Spirit of God say, its time to start planting churches again.

Everything changed that day, as I knew God was going to do something new and incredible. It was not God's will for us to take on the other church, but to step out in faith and start a new church. This church would be a testimony of God's power and faithfulness to give grace to the repentant, and fully restore our lives and ministry.

From that moment, people just started calling me, and asking when I was going to start this new church. I hadn't spoken to anyone, but God was speaking to people. It was on this foundation, and the leading of the Holy Spirit, that Amanda and I knew that God had called us to start the first church in Bangor Maine. After two years, full restoration was not just a thought, theory or a promise, it was becoming a reality!

God has continued to open doors of ministry, and we continue to walk in the ways He has set before us. We have a confidence and belief in God, that our tomorrow will be better than our today. No matter what we have done in the past, if we remain faithful and obedient, God will continue to open doors. I can testify that God restores fully, but my expectation is that God will restore the years we have lost, causing us to touch many more lives in the future, and surpass the things God used us in before.

I want to conclude this chapter with a final look at Peter. Jesus spoke to Peter before he fell, already having a plan for his restoration and future ministry;

> *And the Lord said, "Simon, Simon! Indeed, Satan has asked for you, that he may sift you like wheat, But I have prayed for you that your faith should not fail and when you have returned to me, strengthen your brethren". (Luke 22:31-32)*

This is a remarkable portion of scripture. Jesus deals with the fact that He knew Peter would fall, yet He was already praying for the time he would return. There is so much we can learn from this scripture. The first point we see is that Satan was already after Peter before he fell. I believe Satan knew the force that Peter would be in the future, so he tried to stop him from fulfilling his destiny. Jesus said, *"Satan has asked for you."* This is a New Testament example of that which happened to Job. The enemy saw Job's faithfulness and asked God if he could test him. Like Job, Peter was about to be tested, and because of his arrogance, he didn't believe he could fall. In fact, in the follow verses, he tells Jesus that he would follow Him anywhere.

Peter was naive and foolish in his declaration. I have heard ministers judge other fallen ministers and declare, "I would never be that stupid," and within a short period of time, they have fallen in the same way! The good news is, that the *"gifts and call of God are without repentance." (Romans 11:29)* God knows what He has called us to, and He is not sorry. He knows we would fail before we do, and just like Peter, He still calls us to return to ministry. I firmly believe Jesus is praying for us before we fall, and during our times of disobedience, He desires to see our return, so we can *"strengthen the brethren."* This should cause us to leave our pity parties and jump up and down with excitement! We come to realize that God has always been involved with our lives. Even when they were spinning out of control, He remained in control of our destiny after we fell. All we need to do is submit our lives and ministries to Him, and He will lift us up and set our feet upon the rock and at the right time we will be released again to minister to others.

Chapter 9
HAVING DONE ALL TO STAND, STAND!

It's encouraging to hear amazing stories about how God reaches out to us when we fail. Through His grace, He brings us to a place of recognition and repentance. This starts the restoration process as God takes the broken vessel or our fallen human lives, and starts to remodel us just like the potter who takes the clay and shapes it into a beautiful vessel. He gives us a new purpose, new hope, and a future that looks bright!

This doesn't mean our life and ministry will now be smooth sailing. There are still battles and challenges we have to face. The enemy hates the fact that we can be forgiven and restored in ministry. We have to remember that Satan, who was once called Lucifer, *"son of the morning" (Isaiah 14:14)* fell from his position of ministry because of his greed and need for power. His rebellious heart caused him to be self-centered, and his quest for power led to his downfall. *(Ezekiel 28:11-19)* God never gave Lucifer a chance to repent. There was no plan of redemption, his sin was judged and he will never be forgiven or restored.

Like Lucifer, our fate should be the same. We deserve judgment, we know the truth, and the rules, yet at times we willfully break them. No wonder Satan is mad! He can't understand or comprehend the grace of God. He looks at us, and sees that we have been given another chance, something he never experienced. He thought he had destroyed God's creation when he deceived Adam and Eve, causing them to sin. He had no understanding of God's love for us. He was blindsided by God's mercy and grace that reached out and covered them. With this in mind, its no wonder that he sets himself to do all that he can to undermine our forgiveness. He will not let us move forward without a fight. He will test the truth we hold on to. He will try to afflict our minds with doubt and destroy our faith for the present, and our hope for the future. He will use other people to try and pull us down, as they remind us of our past failures. He will whisper to us about what we can't do! In all this, we have to remember that Satan is the "father of lies", the "accuser of the brethren" and we have to realize our *"fight is not against flesh and blood but principalities and powers"* *(Ephesians 6:12).*

The Apostle Paul tells us that we are in a spiritual battle, and we need to put on the armor of God so we can overcome the lies and plans of the enemy. The enemy will use words, suggestions, people, and he will even twist scripture to try and stop us from fulfilling our potential. Paul encourages us to mark our position and to not give up ground to the enemy, but to stand!

> *Therefore take up the whole amour of God, that you may be able to withstand in the evil day, and having done all to stand. Stand therefore, ... (Ephesians 6:13-14a)*

Our ability to stand in the face of the enemy will determine our future. I have seen people who have fallen because of sin, and no matter how much forgiveness they receive from God, they have an inability to let go of their past and move forward. In sharing my experiences, I prayer that it will help others out of that pit, and get them back on the road to recovery. God has a plan for us and its time that we made a stand and overcome the enemy.

As I was going through the restoration process, God spoke to me frequently. Sometimes it was the still small voice, other times He spoke through the Bible or through people who wanted to help me get back on my feet. However, there were also times that the devil would try to undermine what God was saying. In this chapter, we will look at some of the areas that we have to fight for and to make a stand!

The fight for truth

I am a person that has always loved the Word of God. I believe it is the Truth. It reveals the heart and nature of God, His plan for redemption, and the things that we can do through His power. It's the foundation of what we believe, and how we build our lives. I have always taught that everything we believe must match up with the Word of God.

The Bible tells us that God speaks to us, that we can receive prophetic insight into our future and even receives visions from heaven. However, how do we know that the thoughts we have are from God, or if an insight is true revelation? What about the prophetic word from "Mr. Encouragement?" Is it God inspired, or just the expression of a person's desire for you. What about our visions and dreams? What part of them is from heaven, as opposed to our own imagination? The only true test is to ask if these things match up with the Word of God. If there is something that contradicts God's truth, we need to ditch it. However, if the revelation we have received aligns with God's Word, we can embrace it.

With that kind of truth, we are able to stand against the enemy and be victorious. Paul encourages us to take up the *"sword of the spirit, which is the Word of God" (Ephesians 6:17)* and use it in our fight against the enemy, who is the father of lies. Holding this in mind, we must do everything we can to get a hold of truth.

> *"And you shall know the truth, and the truth shall make you free"* *(John 8:32)*

We can put this scripture another way, *"And you shall know the truth (and the truth that you now know) shall make you free."* No matter what the devil suggests, if the truth is planted in our hearts, we are able to stand and overcome.

During my journey through the wilderness of restoration, people had encouraged me and told me many times that God was not done with me; that He had a greater plan for my future. Their words were encouraging and without them, I would have struggled a lot more. However, I needed more than words; I needed the truth of God's Word. If I could not back up what people were saying with the Word, I had no real foundation upon which I could stand. The good news is that with every step I took towards restoration, God spoke not only into my heart, but confirmed it with scripture. My belief in Gods forgiveness is based on His word. My conviction in His restoration is based on the Word. But, there were two scriptures that caused me problems:

> This is a faithful saying: If a man desires the position of a Bishop, He desires a good work. A Bishop then must be blameless, the husband of one wife….."(I Timothy 3:2)

> If a man is blameless, the husband of one wife….Titus 1;6

Both these scriptures talk about the position of a Bishop or Elder in the church. To be restored as a church leader (which includes pastor, elder and apostle), I needed to understand what the Bible really said. The scriptures clearly state that such a person has to be the "husband of one wife." Many people have interpreted this as, "not divorced." These scriptures caused me great concern. I knew that God had forgiven me, and I believed in restoration, but these scriptures seemed to suggest that full restoration was not possible. Does the divorced minister have to settle for partial restoration because of his or her mistakes?

I knew I had to get a deeper understanding of these passages. The common conclusion did not sit well in my spirit, and it seemed to contradict everything else that was written about God's forgiveness and His desire to fully restore. If I couldn't conclude this matter, it would always be something the enemy could use to restrict full restoration in my life and ministry. It was time to battle for truth. My fight started with every scripture I had read about forgiveness and restoration, all of which pointed to the fact that it was God's intention to fully restore.

The next step was to dig deeper into these scriptures through examination of the original language, the context it was written, and the historic setting of the people receiving the Word. All these aspects help reveal truth. When we look at the Greek language, we see the actual translation is "a one-woman man". The question we have to ask ourselves is, does this literal interpretation challenge some traditional views? We can see why this has been translated as "the husband of one wife," and how we quickly conclude that by this interpretation, it disqualifies anyone who has been divorced. This interpretation has also been taught by some denominations in the church for years. So, when we read it, we come to the same conclusion that they have because that's what we have been told without really further investigating its truths. If this scripture is just talking about a divorced person, why didn't Paul make that clear? He had talked about divorce in the past, and if that were in his mind, you would think that he would just say, "a bishop must be blameless and not divorced." He doesn't say that.

What happens to a person who has been divorced, before they came to Christ? It would come as a surprise if we told the new believer that they were totally forgiven, they had been washed clean, and their sins are remembered no more, except they are now restricted in serving God because of the sin they committed before they came to Christ. Some would argue, that if they got divorced before they became a Christian, this scripture doesn't apply. Well, we can't have it both ways! If it's talking about a divorced person, it doesn't matter whether you were a Christian or not when you got divorced. We either have to accept that we are fully forgiven, or not. If we are fully forgiven, then the price has been paid, and we don't have to continue to pay for our mistakes.

If Paul is only referring to a divorced person, then he has contradicted himself. He has already said in 1 Corinthians 7, that if Christian is married to an unbeliever, and the unbeliever chooses to leave, let them go and get on with your life. We also read in Matthew 5:31-32, that divorce is not acceptable, except where a person commits sexual immorality. It would be a contradiction of scripture, to give people a place where divorce is acceptable, and then restrict that person from being in a specific area of ministry.

There are many people who are victims of divorce. It was not their choice, or desire but it happened. What do we say to the man or woman, who has been cheated on? "I'm sorry for you pain, but now I'm going to add to it and tell you, that you can no longer minister in this position?" If we look at the translation we have before us, it says a bishop must be the "husband of one wife". Well, that stinks for the widower, who has lost their life-long partner, cried their tears, and after a period of time, moved on. To their surprise, they meet someone else. They discover that they can love again, and before long they are married. If we take this portion of scripture that a bishop should be "the husband of one wife," this individual's decision for happiness would put them out of the ministry. We read in Genesis *that it is not good for man to dwell alone". (Genesis 2:8)* Does this statement change if a man or woman is widowed? I do not believe this is the heart of God, as it would deny a person from finding happiness again.

When we look at this scripture in the historical context of when it was written, we realize that Paul lived in a time and culture where five percent of the population practiced polygamy. It was quite common for a man to have more than one wife. In fact, one in every twenty people had more than one wife! This practice is unacceptable to God, and it's unacceptable to a person in a leadership position. Something has to change for that person to be accepted as a good role model and a leader in the church. I believe this is one of the areas the Apostle Paul was talking about.

Polygamy is still practiced in some parts of the world today. One of those places is Nigeria. I found when I ministered there, that it was not unusual for a village chief or leader to have many wives. During the last thirty years, Nigeria has gone through a great transition. Revival has broken out, and Christianity has exploded. Many of the village leaders have come to Christ. Some of them have a great gift to lead, and now they want to use their gifts for the kingdom. The problem is that they have many wives. According to this scripture, they cannot be a bishop or Elder. What should they do? Keep the first wife and divorce the others? If they do that, those who are released are seen as prostitutes, and they are persecuted. The way that many have corrected their former practice of polygamy is to support all of their "wives" financially, but only live as a husband to their first wife. In practice, they become the "husband of one wife" and therefore are positioned to be considered for leadership in the church, if that is what God has anointed and called them to do.

I believe that Paul was writing about polygamy, but that this could also refer to an elder that has fallen into sin by having an affair. Such a person should resign from their position, or resign from their ministry, until the areas of sin are dealt with, and their character defects have been addressed and changed. How about the charismatic flirt, who is not just a one-woman kind of man, but a person that likes to play with the emotions of any woman they come into contact with? Such a person is not qualified to be an elder or bishop in the church, but many people who are like this, have held the position of elder without question or consequence. Again, the character flaws must be addressed and changed.

The question isn't whether you were divorced before you were a Christian. It has nothing to do with a widow who remarries, or a Christian minister who has fallen, it's whether you are a "one-women kind of man" in your present relationship. This scripture addresses the person's present character and lifestyle. How are they living now? If we have remarried after the divorce, are we treating our wives or husbands in a godly, scriptural way? Are our present relationships a good example to the church? If we have repented, and corrected our character defects, and we are living a holy life, I believe you can be fully restored.

Let's take a look at this scripture, and see the qualifications Paul is looking for:

> This is a faithful saying: If a man desires the position of a Bishop, He desires a good work. A bishop then must be blameless, the husband

of one wife (a one-woman man), temperate, sober-minded, of good behavior, hospitable, able to teach, not given to wine, not violent, not greedy for money, but gentle, not covetous; one who rules his own house well, having his children in submission with all reverence (for if a man does not know how to rule his own house, how will he take care of the church of God?"; not a novice, lest being puffed up with pride he fall into the same condemnation as the devil. Moreover, he must have a good testimony among those who are outside, lest he fall into reproach and the snare of the devil. (1 Timothy 3:1-7)

This is a great standard with so many qualifications! I don't know many people who can live up to them all! Even the great Apostle Paul failed at times in areas. We know about his argument with Barnabas in regards to John Mark, and their differing opinions on whether John Mark should assist them on their next ministry trip. This brought division and an abrupt end to their ministry together. *(Acts 15:36-41)* If we measured this moment against Paul's qualifications, he would have been disqualified. He was not gentle, but angry. Maybe there were some violent words that took place. However, God's heart was not to remove his apostleship, but a change of character was necessary in Paul's life.

We can all think of ministers who failed when measured against this standard. Those who are double minded, depending on who they are dealing with, and whether or not they are in the inner circle. Ministers can be hostile instead of hospitable. Some will never invite you to their home, or out for a meal. There are those who do nothing but eat meal after meal, and their sermons are only about money, money and more money. Is that not greed? We have the minister who is a control freak, barking orders and demanding this and that, and when you make a small mistake, they become derailed and violent! No signs of gentleness there! And everyone knows that pastor's kids are usually poorly behaved, disrespectful, and uncontrollable. We have all fallen short of this list, so does that mean no one should be in the position of bishop or elder?

I am not trying to disguise one person's sin by elevating another person's mistake. I just want us to have an honest understanding of this scripture. We all fall short, and we all need to repent, and adjust our character. If there is something that cannot be addressed quickly, and the person's sin becomes a lifestyle, then that person needs to be rested from ministry until such a time that they repent and change. Once this has taken place, they can experience full restoration.

The conclusion in my battle for truth is simple. If you have sinned, you need to repent and accept the forgiveness of God. Once forgiven, the restoration process begins, and it continues until we are fully restored. The enemy will at times challenge this belief and even send some people to argue another opinion. It's in those times that we have to take hold of truth, and having done all, to stand. The Word of God is a powerful weapon. We have not been called to be men-pleasers, but we have been called to serve God. God loves to take the *"weak things of this world to confound the wise"*. Are we ready to take a stand and place ourselves in the midst of the battle for the sake of the Kingdom of God?

Clearing the "mind" field

The next area in which we need to stand is against every lie, thought and imagination that tries to attack our mind. Our thoughts are like bombs that have been strategically placed by an enemy in a minefield, whose purpose is to destroy us! The wrong thoughts and imaginations that we allow to live and grow in our mind become a detonator that triggers an explosion or reaction in our lives. If we do not deal with our wrongful thinking, and fail to defuse the bomb, there will be an explosion that will lead to our destruction. (As a play on words, we will call the minefield, a "Mind field"). I was once told that I was too young to minister, and that it was impossible to start a church with three people and see it succeed. That was a man's opinion. I could have allowed this other person's thoughts to affect my thinking and detonate an imagination of failure. If I had allowed that to happen, I would never have started the church in Bristol, or seen the great things that God performed.

I have always been a positive thinker. There has never been a challenge that was too big or a problem that could not have been overcome. In fact, I live for the challenge of doing the things that people say are impossible! I serve a miracle working God, and whatever looks impossible in the natural, is just a small mountain to God that can be easily moved and cast into the sea. Although I had faced many challenges, problems and difficult situations I had never thought about defeat, until I went through my divorce. My foundational belief in God's favor, His anointing, and supernatural power to change situations, was now undermined by the fact that I had chosen to do things my way. I felt like I no longer deserved God to work and move on my behalf. Even after I had truly repented, and did all that I could do to live righteously, I had to learn to take control of my mind again.

Everyday, my thoughts and imagination were bombarded with visions of failure. Fear clouded my faith. Condemnation overwhelmed my soul, and at times I even questioned my salvation. The enemy would tell me that I had no future, my dreams were broken, and there was no way back into ministry. There were days that I was able to take the Word of God and stand against the lies of the enemy, but there were other days that his attacks against my mind were ruthless and I would find myself worn out, feeling overwhelmed and depressed.

But suddenly, the battle turned in my favor. One morning, as I was walking our dog (a 160 pound Great Dane), God spoke into my heart and reminded me that I was in a spiritual battle. He told me that I needed to take control against the thoughts and imagination in my mind. Then, He dropped this word into my heart, "that the enemy could only destroy my life, if I believed and responded to his suggestions. However, He (Jesus) could only rebuild my life, if I responded to His words of truth and His encouragement. I realized that I could no longer be *"double minded and tossed around like the waves of the sea," (James 1:6-8)* but I had to choose who I was going to listen to, and make a stand.

It doesn't matter how powerful we think the devil is. He is not in control of our future, unless we believe his words, and allow him to influence our thinking, and therefore, restrict our future. On the other hand, God is all-powerful and our destiny is in His hands. It is God who has called us, placed gifts in our lives and a dream in our heart. But, He has also given us a free will. No matter how much God speaks to us, or we allow people to prophecy over us, our destiny will only be unlocked when we take God at His word and step out in faith. We have to believe what God is saying about us and do all we can to move forward towards the goals He has put in our hearts. We have to win the battle of the mind!

The way we think about ourselves defines who we are in the present, and it determines what we will or won't do in the future. Our thoughts shape the way we see ourselves and how we presume others see us. Those thoughts affect the way we act. If we truly believe God has forgiven us for the mistakes we have made, we will have a positive outlook about ourselves. We won't care how other people see us because we know we are right with God. However, if we believe the lies of the enemy that we have not been forgiven, we feel defeated and may struggle to even go to church. We will be afraid about what people may think or say to us. Our thinking affects our self-image. This causes us to take our eyes off of God, and His promises, and causes us to focus on ourselves and the mistakes we have made. The scripture says:

"For as he thinks in his heart, so is he" (Proverbs 23:7)

When we look at the life of King David, we see that he was a very positive thinker. He knew who he was and the God he served. He had an incredible record of success in war. He never lost a battle and he came through every challenge victorious. What gave him the ability to do this? It was the way he saw himself, and his foundational beliefs about who he was, based on what God said about him.

Let's look at David's most famous battle against Goliath. This giant of a man came out against King Saul and the people of Israel. Now King Saul was not a short man. He was head and shoulders above the rest *(1 Samuel 9:2)* and he was the anointed king of Israel. God was on his side, and the people of Israel were ready to fight for him. Saul should have taken his rightful place as the leader of Israel at the front of the battle-line, and he should have led the army into victory as they defeated the enemy. We know this didn't happen, and the reason is because he believed the lies of the enemy. *(1 Samuel 17:8-12)* The enemy's words created images, which caused the king and the people to fear. Their fear determined their action. Instead of fighting, they ran and hid for fear of their lives. *"As a man thinks, so is he"* If we think we will be defeated, we act in a defeated manner and hide. We will fail to face the challenges of life and we will be overcome.

David was different. His mind was strong because his belief was in God. When David heard what had happened, his response was to find the king, and declare his desire to go up against Goliath. King Saul did not believe David could defeat the giant, but David would not take no for an answer. His response was simple:

> But David said to Saul, "Your servant used to keep his fathers sheep, and when a lion or a bear came and took a lamb out of the flock, I went out after it and struck it and delivered the; lamb from its mouth; and when it arouse against me, I caught it by its beard and struck and killed it. Your servant has killed both lion and bear, and this uncircumcised Philistine will be like one of them, seeing he has defiled the armies of the living God" (1 Samuel 17:34-36)

David's belief in himself and the God he served produced positive thinking and an act of bravery that elevated him in the eyes of Israel. When he went out against Goliath and defeated him, he stopped being a boy in the eyes of others, and became a man. His thinking created an action that changed his future. He not only overcame the Goliath, but as a direct result, he was made the captain over the armies of Israel. *(1 Samuel 18:13)* A positive attitude based on God's Word brings promotion. When we have the right kind of thinking, there is no giant that can stand in our way, or no skeleton from our past, that can restrict our future. Do we believe in God's redemptive power to forgive and cleanse us, or do we listen to the lies of the enemy? The biggest giant we will face in our lives is wrong thinking!

Another thing we see about David's attitude is that his thinking was framed by his understanding of God. When King Saul tried to talk David into walking away, David pointed out how he saw Goliath – "uncircumcised" and therefore, outside of the covenant or favor and covering of God's power. David, on the other hand, was a child of God. He was circumcised on the eight day after his birth. *(Genesis 17:10)* Every child that was born in Israel was to be circumcised. It spoke of the covenant that God made with his people, and the promises that came with that covenant. He believed the promise that God would bless, give favor, protect, and go before him in battle, fighting on his behalf. God would give him the power to overcome. David knew the difference between the enemy, Goliath, and himself. David was a child of God, whom God had promised to keep and go before him. Goliath, was an enemy to the children of Israel, God's people and therefore an enemy not just of David but also of God. David knew the battle would be easy, God was on his side and that guaranteed the victory.

The verbal exchange between David and Goliath, reflects the way David thought, and caused him to be confident in his pursuit of his enemy.

> *And when the Philistine looked about and saw David, he distained him, for he was only a youth, ruddy and good looking. So the philistine said to David, "Am I a dog, that you come to me with sticks?"*

And the Philistine cursed David by his gods. And the philistine said to David, "Come to me and I will give your flesh to the birds of the air and the beasts of the field!" Then David said to the philistine, you come to me with a sword, with a spear and with a javelin, But I come to you in the name of the Lord of hosts, the God of the armies of Israel, whom you defiled. This day the Lord will deliver you into my hands, and I will strike you and take your head from you. And this day I will give the carcasses of the camp of the Philistines to the birds of the air and the wild beasts of the earth, that all the earth may know there is a God in Israel" (1 Samuel 17:42-46)

I love this confidence! David's knowledge of his God framed his thinking and his actions. The Bible says *"My people are destroyed for lack of knowledge"* (Hosea 4:6) Are we allowing the way we think to effect our lives? We need to get God's thinking, His words and truth, to perforate our imaginations. If we are going to stand, we have to create a strong foundation. If the enemy is ripping our hearts apart with accusations regarding our past mistakes, we need to focus on what God says about us. Most people, when they are afraid, do what King Saul did, they run from the enemy and hide. We can't hide from our past mistakes. They can be a giant in our lives if we allow people to try and use them against us. But, if we have the knowledge of who God is, and what He has done, we will have a positive outlook. We will not run from our accusers, but with truth, we will be able to stand and overcome.

I want to re-establish the point in which began this section. People are not our enemy. *"Our fight is not against flesh and blood but principalities and powers."* (Ephesians 6:12) It is the lies of the enemy that fills peoples' minds and causes them to be judgmental. They may not have an understanding of grace. Our job is not to retaliate; they are not our enemy but our brother or sister in Christ. However, we do have a real enemy, the devil, and we need to come against him. He is a goliath, who will accuse and do all he can to intimidate us. Sometimes, he will use other people, and sometimes he will fill our minds with negative thoughts or imaginations. We have to make a stand and fight if we are to be fully restored. The Bible tells us that we have the power to overcome:

> *For though we walk in the flesh, we do not war according to the flesh, for the weapons of our warfare are not carnal but mighty in God for pulling down of strongholds, casting down arguments and every high thing that exalts itself against the knowledge of God, bringing every thought into captivity to the obedience of Christ. (2 Corinthians 10:3-5)*

This scripture not only reveals the power God has given us in defeating the enemy, but also the way in which the enemy works. If an army knows the strategies and plans of its enemy, it weakens the enemy's attack. We will have the upper hand in the battle against the lies of the enemy, if we do not walk after the flesh, but claim our spiritual weapons.

This scripture talks about arguments, and every high thing that exalts itself against the knowledge of God. We all struggle with thoughts, imaginations, lies, mental pictures, speculations and pretensions from time to time. But the way the enemy works, is that he wants to build a "stronghold" in our mind. So, what is this stronghold, and how do we bring it down?

The Greek word for "stronghold" in the context of this scripture, refers to a "castle or fortress of thought," that the enemy seeks to establish in the minds of believers. It's the "arguments and reasons by which a dispute endeavors to fortify the enemy's opinion, and he defends it against his opponent", us! Imagine what a castle looks like to the enemy. It is strong, fortified, and an unassailable stronghold, which holds us prisoner. It's of rugged construction, laid one brick at a time, and there is no easy way in or out. That's what the enemy wants to do in your mind. This is how it works. The Father of lies makes a suggestion to you, such as, "You will never be fully restored or as successful as you were in the past." That first suggestion, is the first brick in the building of a stronghold or castle in our mind. The next thing he does, is influence a fellow believer to speak to us, and they suggest that our "best days are behind us," or that we "will never get the chance to do that again." This suggestion is the next brick in the stronghold, and so the construction continues with the enemy's suggestions and people's words. Before long, it a stronghold in our minds. It affects our thinking and restricts what we do in the future. All we can see are the lies that have been spoken, and now we are trapped in this stronghold of thought. This "stronghold "of thought is an attack against the knowledge of God. So, how do we overcome? We have to get knowledge! What does God say? What does His Word say? What is the Spirit of God stirring up in our hearts? It's God's truth, and His Word, that become the weapons of warfare. They are mighty in God, given to us to use when we face the enemy to pull down those lies and strongholds!

The Goliath we face today is no different to the one King David faced. We may not see him, but his accusations are the same, and he seeks to intimidate us in the same way he tried to intimidate David. We need to have the same mind as David, and be encouraged in our fight for the future. Every Christian, leader or minister, who has fallen from grace, sinned, gone through a divorce or any other area of failure, will be faced with the challenge of getting back up and fighting for their future. I found myself in this place, and although at times it is intimidating and frightening, I chose to stand on the Word of God. Every time the enemy lied to me, or created wrong thinking, I made a stand and declared truth.

The enemy will tell us that we chose to sin, to get a divorce or that it was our fault so we are outside of God's mercy. God tells us *"where sin abounds, Grace much more."* I like to put it this way; where there's more sin, God gives much more grace *(Romans 5:20)*. The enemy will tell us that our mistakes are too great, our sin will place a black mark over us for the rest of our lives. Maybe the enemy is lying about our future and that we are beyond full restoration. That your days of being used by God are in the past and your hopes and dreams are shattered forever!

God says, *"As far as the east is from the west, So far has He removed our transgressions from us"* (Psalm 103:12).

I love the God we serve. He hates that we have sinned but He loves to restore and give hope for the future. Our sin is not stronger than the call of God. His purpose remains the same, *"For the gifts and the calling of God are irrevocable or without repentance"* (Romans 11:29). God is not repentant, or sorry that He called us, He just has to reshape us to fulfill His purposes in our lives. The heart of God is to reach out and reshape the fallen individual. God calls out to the *"spiritual to restore such a one (who has been overtaken by sin) in a spirit of gentleness, considering yourself, lest you also be tempted."* (Galatians 6:1)

When we fall and make ungodly decisions, we are seen to be foolish in the eyes of other believers. We are seen as ministers who have made stupid decisions, and in many ways they are right. However we have just become candidates for God's grace, for He loves to take *"the foolish things of this world to put to shame the wise and God has chosen the weak things of the world to put to shame the things which are mighty"* (1 Corinthians 1:27). In regards to our future, we may have low expectations, feeling we don't deserve much, but God's opinion is different than ours. God says, *"For I know the thoughts that I think towards you, says the Lord, thoughts of peace and not of evil, to give you a future and a hope."* The New International version puts it this ways, *"For I know the plans I have for you, plans to prosper you and not to harm you, plans to give you hope and a future"* (Jeremiah 29:11)

Whose report are we going to believe? The one the enemy tells us, or what God says about us. It's time to make a stand on a strong foundation of Biblical truth, and overcome the lies and imaginations of the enemy. We need to shake ourselves out of our pity party! It's time to speak truth into our lives and remove the fear and doubt that is holding us back! We matter to the kingdom of God and we have a purpose in the church today. Make a stand!

Fighting for our future!

I love the prophetic gifts God has given to the church. Whether we see them ministered through the office of a prophet *(Ephesians 4:11)*, or through the gift of prophecy *(1 Corinthians 12:10)*, that has been given to the body for our encouragement and edification. When we receive a word from God in this manner, it lifts our spirit and causes us to take our eyes off of our present situations, so we can see things the way God sees them. I know many prophets are eccentric, and the manner they deliver God's Word sometimes seems odd. This may cause some people to back off, and doubt if what is said is from God. When we look at scripture, and see prophetic figures, many of them are a little strange. John the Baptist lived in a wilderness, eating locusts and wild honey, yet when God moved him he moved a nation to repentance.

There are people in the church, who love the gift of prophecy, and at every opportunity they try to pray for you, and speak "God's Word" into your life. Many of us have had good and bad experiences. We may think that the word given was accurate, and other times we wonder which god they are listening to! It causes us to walk away wondering what is this "gift" of prophecy. If we strip away the man-part, and their over enthusiasm to be used of God to encourage a fellow Christian, there is something deep and meaningful that happens that is of God.

The reason I am talking about prophecy this way is because where we are in our relationship with God, determines how we receive a prophetic word. When we are walking in obedience, and achieving things in the ministry, we accept the prophetic word more readily than when we are struggling with our walk with God. It is when everything is difficult that we question prophetic words, and wonder if they were from God. When we have fallen, sinned, or gone through a moral failure, we are left wondering what all those prophetic words were about. We look at our present conditions, and if they don't line up with the things God has said about us, we begin to question.

Some people say that prophetic words are conditional. Fulfillment is based on our obedience. When God speaks, and we walk in obedience, we see the desired outcome. To a certain extent I agree. However, if God knows all things as the Bible declares, He also knew the mistakes we would make, and the areas of disobedience we would walk into. So knowing that, why would He inspire people to speak these prophetic words into our lives before we walked in disobedience, if He knew they would never be fulfilled? Is this God just being God, who looks beyond our past and present weaknesses, and sees our potential in the future? If so, we need to take hold of the very prophetic words we struggle with, due to our mistakes and use them to stand and fight for our God given destiny.

One of the awesome things about God is that He sees beyond the place we are at the present time. A great example of this can be seen in the book of Judges, when God speaks to Gideon, and calls him a *"mighty man of valor!" (Judges 6:12)* Gideon had great potential, but at the time God called out to him he was far from the "mighty man of valor" that God spoke about. He was a cynical, hurt individual, who was struggling to believe what God said about him. Does it sound familiar?

Gideon had seen the armies of Midian advance against Israel for seven years *(Judges 6:1)*. They were consistently killing the people, stealing the harvest and leaving Israel to suffer in the wake of defeat. Not only had there been national loss, but he had suffered personal loss through his brothers being killed by the enemy *(Judges 8:18-19)*. He was reeling with grief and questioning God. When God spoke to Gideon, he was hiding in a wine press *(Judges 6:11)*, questioning the prophetic word. He even wondered if God was with Israel, and asks, "Where are all God's (so called) miracles, which our fathers told us about?" *(Judges 6:13)* Then he makes a further suggestion that, *"The Lord has forsaken us and delivered us into the hands of the Midianites." (Judges 6:14).* It is obvious to see that Gideon is struggling with the word he has received. He does not see things the way God sees them. He doubts that he could ever be the hero of the hour, because in his view he is from the *"weakest family in Manasseh" (Judges 6:15)* Yet in the midst of all his hurt and fear, God's word still stands. God spoke to Gideon's future. He was, and he would be seen as, "a mighty man of valor."

I have noticed that God usually speaks a prophetic word into our lives when we feel weak, defeated, or we are questioning our future. When we are feeling victorious, strong, and full of faith, we don't need those words of inspiration as we already feel inspired. When Gideon chose to listen and believe the things that God said about him, he opened his life to the Spirit of God, and the anointing of the Holy Spirit fell on him. This enabled him to do all the things God said he would do, and he became the man God said he would become. *(Judges 6:34)*

We are no different than Gideon. We have been in positions of weakness, whether they resulted from our own mistakes or from the decisions others have made and we have suffered losses and grief. We may be cynical, and struggling to believe the things God has said about us, but the moment we start listening to God and take our eyes off the situation we are in, we start to see things through the eyes of God. This enables us to open our lives to the Holy Spirit again, and experience His power and anointing. We are able to stand against the enemy and establish the kingdom of God.

We need the prophetic word if we are going to stand and fight for our future. The Apostle Paul told Timothy that the gifts of prophecy are a weapon of warfare:

> *This charge I commit to you, son Timothy, according to the prophecies previously made concerning you, that by them you may wage a good warfare. (I Timothy 1:18)*

Timothy was a young minister who faced opposition from inside, and outside the church. Paul was encouraging him, not to be distracted, but to stand and fight. And the way to fight was by using the prophetic words given to him. Paul was saying, "Timothy, wake up to what has God said to you, what His words and promises are in your life. Stop listening to people's opinion and attacks. Listen to God. Stand on the foundation of truth that He has given you, and fight for your future!" We can all heed this charge. When we fail, the last thing we want to do is fight. All we see is the mess we have made, and we wonder if there is any future. God has spoken to us and He wants us to get back on our feet. The way we do this is by taking hold of the prophetic words.

When I was going through my season of restoration, God moved me to read what had been prophetically spoken over my life. I was stirred to re-read all the scriptural promises that were the foundation of my calling and ministry. The more I read, and meditated on them, the more I realized that the words that had been spoken into my life then, remained true in the present. I was able to take these things as a foundation of prayer and in my battle against the lies of the enemy.

One of the biggest questions I had when reviewing scriptures and prophecies I had received over the years was, which ones were still applicable, and which ones were no longer valid? The other challenge I found myself facing was the fact that God had told me to marry Laura, and we had received many prophetic words together. What was I to do with those words?

First, I had to come to terms with the fact that I had stepped out of the will of God in my marriage to Laura, and by doing so, there were consequences. These are not the same as unforgiveness. God forgives the sin, and by His grace He reshapes us, and gives us a new beginning. One of the consequences was, that some promises from God that were made between Laura and me, had now been cut off due to my disobedience. In this area, I believe that prophetic words are conditional based on our obedience. There is nothing I can do to resurrect some of those words. They were for both of us, as we walked in ministry together. The moment we stopped walking together, the prophetic words were cut off. I have to accept that there is a price in making mistakes.

However, just because some words are cut off, does not mean all the words are cut off. If we are gifted in an area, God will still use the gift, but it may take a different journey. One of the prophetic words that Laura and I received on numerous occasions, was that we would write together and produce manuscripts, training material and books. This prophetic word came true, as we produced material for The Apostolic School of Ministry, seminars and leadership training. In this area, we excelled in God's blessing and anointing. I am gifted to write, and Laura was gifted in editing. Her grasp of the English language was amazing. When we were married, this was an area that came easily to us, but once we were divorced, this prophetic word was cut off. We were no longer together, we lived three thousand miles apart and we no longer wanted to write together.

Just because that prophetic word to Laura and me had been cut off, didn't mean that God had taken away my gift or desire to write. It was still part of God's desire for my prophetic destiny, but the way it was going to be fulfilled would be different. I needed to find someone else who would do the editing, and all the other hard work of correcting my grammar! God has obviously met that need, as this book is part of God's prophetic destiny in my life. So, when we look at the things God has spoken to us, it is important that we don't "throw out the baby with the bathwater!" The environment and circumstances may change, and the dynamic of gifts may differ, but God's prophetic word in our lives doesn't change. There is the new challenge of accepting our weaknesses, and finding other solutions to the challenges we face in fulfilling our prophetic destiny.

Once we understand this, there is something else to consider. God is great at giving us new beginnings. Just because I had stepped out of the will of God through my divorce from Laura, didn't mean that God wanted me to live the rest of my life single, or working the ministry on my own. God' says *"It is not good for man to dwell alone; I will make him a helper comparable to him." (Geneses 2:18)* If this is true, before we walk in disobedience, it is still true after. I know God has given me a new beginning with Amanda. In giving me Amanda, I believe she is a *"helper"* who is *"comparable"* to me. Or, as some translations put it, *"a completing partner."* In our marriage we have now become the team God wants us to become. We are a new family unit that God can use for His purposes. A great example of this is how God used David and Bathsheba, to bring a son named Solomon to be a son of promise, and prophetic fulfillment in the House of Israel.

Now, with this new family and new beginning, there is a mixture of new and different gifts. The gifts that God has placed in my life have not changed, but Amanda has gifts that are different to me. When we put them together, a new dynamic takes place. So, even though some prophetic words have been cut off, Amanda and I are now in a position to receive new prophetic words, that speak of our future and ministry together in the Kingdom.

Finally, there are prophetic words that have been given to us, either before we were married, or during our marriages, but they were specifically for the individual. God has called each of us and if we stand on the truth of His Word, and step out in faith, these words will still come to pass. The mistakes we have made or the situations we find ourselves in, due to other people's mistakes, have not altered the words we have received. Let me give you a few examples:

Abram received a prophetic word at the grand age of seventy-five. God promised him that he would become a "Great Nation." *(Genesis 12:1-4)* The problem presented is that Sarah, his wife, is advanced in years and unable to bear children. This isn't a great problem because we serve a miracle working God, who can change things around and create something out of nothing. The challenge we face is being patient. When things don't work out in the time frame we think it should, we can become fearful and start to take matters into our own hands.

This happened to Abram. After a period of time of waiting, he becomes afraid because he has no offspring *(Geneses 15:1-3)*. God tells him not to fear, and speaks prophetically into his life again. Then, Sarah struggles with the word God had given, and suggests that Abram takes her maidservant, Hagar. We don't see any struggle from Abram, and as quickly as the suggestion has been made, he agrees and sleeps with Hagar! Their plan works, but with consequences. Hagar gets pregnant and nine months later, Ishmael is born. This was not God's plan for the promised son, and their disobedience created jealousy, and conflicts within Abram's family.

God is faithful and gracious. He speaks prophetically into Abrams life again, and in doing so changes his name from Abram to Abraham, which is translated "father of many nations." *(Geneses 17:5)* After twenty-four years, Abraham is on board with God's plan. His wife, Sarah, will give birth to the son of promise. But, Sarah is still struggling with unbelief *(Geneses 18:12)*. There may have been a time in the beginning that she believed this word, but now she was a lot older, and thought it was impossible.

We all know the outcome of the prophetic word. God was right, and the word came to pass:

> And the Lord visited Sarah as He had said, and the Lord did for Sarah as He had spoken. For Sarah conceived and bore Abraham a son in his old age, at the set time of which God had spoken to him. *(Genesis 21:1-2)*

God did as "He had spoken" The fulfillment of the prophetic word was not in Abraham and Sarah's hands, but God's. In their doubt, they tried to develop their own plan and thereby sinned against God. Abram had slept with another women, yet their disobedience did not stop God from doing what He had promised at the "set time." It is in this area, that I disagree with the belief that some Christians have concerning prophetic words being conditionally based on obedience. Both Abraham and Sarah were disobedient in their walk before God, specifically in the area they were called to in creating a son of promise, and the birth of a nation called Israel. Yet, God was still faithful to His prophetic word. We may struggle to understand this, but it's still in the Bible. This is what makes God so great, and "His ways higher than our ways". We may have sinned and walked in disobedience, but many of the prophetic words we have been given by God remain. He gave them before we fell, and they remain in tact once we are restored. If we can grab hold of this truth, we can use those prophetic words as weapons of warfare to stand against the lies of the enemy and walk victoriously.

Another example of this, is for people who are the victims of another's mistakes. For those people who never wanted to get divorced, and fought for their marriages, the choices of their partner left them in the same place as those who initiated the divorce. They suffer great loss, grieve, and their world is turned upside down. If they were married to someone and shared in the ministry, they feel they have had a setback in what God has called them to do. They may wonder what will happen to those words that were received and if they will ever be fulfilled.

There are two people in the Bible, I love to read and talk about, Caleb and Joshua. These were men of great character and faith. They were almost ahead of their time in the way they thought, and in the way they saw the future. As we know, they were part of the twelve spies, who were sent by Moses to check out the Promised Land. They were to bring back a report that would be encouraging for the Children of Israel to move forward and possess the promises of God. Unfortunately, the other spies that went with them didn't have the same vision as Caleb or Joshua. They struggled to see the future, and the potential of the Promised Land. They got caught up with what was happening in the present, and all they could see were the obstacles, or giants in the land. *(Numbers 13)*

So often we focus on the things we are going through today. We get caught up with everyday life, or the challenges we face. If we only see the immediate challenges, those things consume our attention and thinking. This is not how God wants us to focus. He will guide us through the challenges of the day, and at the same time He will give us a vision for the future.

When the twelve spies reported back to Moses, ten of them gave him a bad report. Only Caleb and Joshua spoke positively. Unfortunately, Moses and the people were consumed with the things they heard men say rather than the things God was saying. I am sure you have been there! This caused them to doubt their potential, and their fear caused them to reject God's Word *(Number 14:11)*. This resulted in them spending the rest of their lives in the wilderness. Now, this is a case, where the prophetic is conditional. The word will not come to pass in our lives if God speaks, and we choose to walk away, without ever repenting, or doing anything with the gifts God has given us. This act of stubbornness and self-will, obviously will stop that prophetic word from coming to pass in our lives. Only true repentance can kick start the promises again. The good news is, that there were two people in the camp who believed God's Word. God had promised to give Israel their own land, and He would do it by using these faithful servants, and everyone under the age of twenty, to take possession of it. *(Numbers 14 26-30)*

We may look at Caleb and Joshua and feel sorry for them. They were ready the first time they spied out the land, but because of other people's choices, they too found themselves in the wilderness for forty years. This is just like those who are experiencing the casualties of divorce. The promise and purpose of God did not change towards them, and it does not change towards us. The time frame may be altered, or different to our original thinking, but the prophetic word remains the same, and it will come to pass. The important thing for us to remember is that we cannot allow bitterness, or any other thing, to take hold of our hearts while we are going through this waiting period. God wants us ready when the time comes for the release of His promises

When the time came, Joshua and Caleb were ready, and they led the Children of Israel out of the wilderness into the Promised Land. Their faith was as strong as the first time they spied out the land. They were not afraid of the giants, or the obstacles, and with great belief in God, they were victorious in possessing the land, giving Israel a home in which the blessings of God could be poured out. *(Book of Joshua)*

As we conclude this chapter, there is much that we can be encouraged about. We live in a world where we often make mistakes, or other peoples' choices affect us, but we have to keep our eyes on the Jesus. His plans and purposes do not change. He knows the world we live in, and the mistakes that we will make, and yet He still speaks prophetically into our hearts.

Even as I write this chapter, Amanda and I face opposition from an individual who struggles with the grace that God has towards us. That person fails to understand God's love, and His desire to open doors for us to minister. He tries, with his human efforts, to disrupt the plans and purposes of God by calling local ministers and speaking things that are not true, trying to get them to disassociate themselves from us. Now the challenge we have, is to stand on the Word of God, and the prophetic promises God has made towards us. Our flesh wants to confront the situation and try to bring order, but our faith calls us to focus on what God is saying, and not looking at what man is doing. We are faced with the question, "Do we believe it's God who opens doors and gives favor?" If so, no man can close them. We are left with the conviction that

God is in control, and we realize that *"our fight is not against flesh and blood,"* and God has commanded us to *"pray for our enemies."* (Matthew 5:44) Over the last few weeks, knowing what the enemy has been trying to do, we have found that pastors have called us, to warn us about the things that this individual is doing. Our response is to stand on the prophetic and written word and pray. As we have done this, God has continued to open doors to us. These are the very doors that the enemy has tried to close. God is not only good, He is great!

Now it's your choice. Today is not about the mistakes we have made, or the injustices that has been made towards us. Will we believe the things that God is saying, and will we start fighting for our future? Our future is as promising today, as the day we became a Christian, but we have to choose to see life God's way. We will face many obstacles in life because there is a real enemy, the devil, and there are people who don't see things from our perspective. We may face a few extra obstacles because of the choices we have made, but our trust is in God and His ability to give favor, and open doors. We are all in need of God's strength and power. We just need to learn to stand in faith, and *"having done all to stand, stand!"*

Chapter 10
BE STILL!

Have you ever called out to get the attention of a child that's running around the house making lots of noise? Efforts are in vain, as the child's excitement increases. They may start jumping on the dog, (who in our case is a 160 pound Great Dane, that can knock you out with a quick, unexpected turn of his head), or the noise level rises as the other kids get frustrated because they can't watch their favorite show. You can't hear yourself think! All you want to do, is make the child stop, and "be still" for a moment so they can hear your instructions. This is our fun loving, and at times, chaotic home which I expect is not too different from others! This image of a child at home, jumping and screaming is a reflection of how we are in our world. We run around doing all that we have to do, trying to keep up with the demands of life, and all God wants us to do is "be still." He needs us to be able to listen so He can give us useful instructions to help us on this journey of restoration.

Building relationship

This book, has been a testament of my journey of restoration. For me it has been a wilderness, in which there have been lessons to learn. One of the greatest lessons we need to learn is, if we are going to once again run after the things of God, we have to learn to "be still". This is a paradox, but our understanding of this truth really unlocks our future. The psalmist wrote:

"Be still and know that I am God" (Psalm 46:10)

Our world is cluttered with work, responsibilities, family life, and ministry. For those of us who have made mistakes, we also have to deal with our past, and the destruction we have left behind. We are trying to mend broken dreams at the same time we are endeavoring to make sense of God and the future He promises. It's a whirlwind of activity, and God wants us to "be still," so He can have relationship with us and guide us forward.

As we read about people who go into the wilderness, we understand that there are obstacles to overcome, but we also realize that this is a time of seclusion. It's a time when we are cut off from some of the activities that drive us to do the things we did before. Some of the friends we once had are no longer around. The church programs we were involved in, no longer exist and there is a moment in our life when we are less active. What can God do with this time? When we look at Jesus and His time in the wilderness, He chose to fast for forty days. *(Matthew 4)* What was the purpose of this? When we choose to fast, we give up our natural desires, and call on God. We learn to wait, listen, and seek answers to prayer or direction from the Father. It's during this time, that our rebellious, independent nature is submitted to God, and we become interdependent with Him. We start to move in tangent with the Father's will. It's the place of relationship and trust.

There is so much that God wants to tell us or guide us in, but we are too busy doing a thing our way. Just think about our "quiet times" before the Lord. When was our last time with Him? Was it really quiet? Some people call their prayer times their "quiet time," and they do everything *but* be quiet. As Christians, we spend a lot of time asking God for things, and telling God what His Word says, and we make demands based on our belief, but how much time do we really spend in quiet and listening to the Father? If we will take the time to wait, rest and listen, we will hear God's Word, His heart, and the hope He has for us. When the Psalmist says, *"Be still,"* it literally means to *"let go, to cease from striving, to wait and keep waiting and to be silent"*. This can be an extremely difficult thing to do. I know what I believe, and I'm quick to tell this to God. I know what I want to do, and I like to let God know. I love being busy, and the activity of life thrills me, driving me on to the next thing. However, in recent years, God has worked on me and I am learning to be still, and listen to Him.

God loves relationship and He loves to talk with His children. I have taught for years about how God speaks to us in our everyday lives, and how we need to have a close relationship with Him. We don't need to be in a church service to talk to or hear from God. I have taught that we can speak to God while we're driving, doing the laundry, cooking a meal or just going about our everyday activities. Even though this is true, there are times when we need to just be still, and rest at the feet of Jesus. What would our relationship be like with our spouse if we only spoke with each other while doing other things? If we never sat down, and talked, or never had a date night, it would be difficult to grow into a productive relationship. There are times when we need to cease from what we are doing and be still to create a better future.

If we are going to be successful in getting through our wilderness experience, and enter into the Promised Land of God, we need to learn to rest. During this journey, we will face many obstacles, and our lives need to have a relationship with God as its foundation:

> But those who wait on the Lord, Shall renew their strength, they shall mount up with wings like eagles, they shall run and not be weary, they shall walk and not faint. (Isaiah 40:31)

If the promise of strength is for those who wait, then the opposite, weakness, is true for those who don't wait. We will not have our strength renewed. We will not be able to run, because we will remain weary from the trials of life. Those who have gone through a divorce, have endured an awful ordeal. No matter how much counseling, or words of encouragement we may have received, our wounds will continue to bleed, affecting us and those around us, if we fail to let God back into our lives to help us. In order to let God into our comfort zone, we have to cease doing things our way, which is probably what got us into trouble in the first place. We need to learn to wait for God's direction, and impartation, allowing Him to direct, guide, and renew our strength for life.

There have been many times during my journey that I have wanted to defend myself and speak out against those who have judged me. I have wanted to give my opinions about restoration, but while we are being restored, it not time to speak. Our words can be defensive and may cause more harm than good. It's better to leave those things in the hands of God, and concentrate on the things that God is saying to us. This does not mean that the journey is easy, or that we will make it through without a fight. There are so many obstacles, we may feel like we are going from one battle to the next. It may be a battle for our sanity, or the respect of our children. It may be a battle for relationship, or just to get up and go to work in the morning. There are many natural and supernatural battles, that take place. How are we to survive the continuous turmoil and attacks that present themselves?

King David wrote one of the most famous psalms in the Bible. Most people have heard its words, or they have sung the psalm, *"The Lord is my Shepherd" (Psalm 23)*. David sings this song to the Lord, in a very personal way. He calls out to God as, *"My Shepherd"*, reflecting his personal experience of relationship with the Father. The psalm overflows with peace, as we imagine the green pastures, and picture David being led beside the still waters, having his soul restored. We then read of David's reassurance, of God being with him in the midst of the shadow of death. We all need this comfort when we walk through the dark times in our lives. Then he sings these next words:

> *You prepare a table before me in the presence of my enemies. (Psalm 23:5)*

Wow, I just love this image! This is a reflection of "being still "and waiting on God, in the midst of a chaotic battle. How did David get to this place of "being still" at the table of the Lord, in the midst of a great battle, unless he experienced it? We know that David was a great warrior, and yet he never presumed he knew the answer or the strategy for victory. We see him on many occasions, calling out to God, asking for direction and anointing before the battle. (*1 Samuel 23:4, 1 Samuel 30:8, 2 Samuel 5:19 & 23*)

These scriptures are examples of David "being still" in the midst of the battle. So, whether it was before, or during a battle, David knew the secret of "being still" and waiting on God. We can only imagine the pressure on King David, to lead and give direction to his army, and to be at the forefront of the battle. He was setting an example of his trust in God to keep him alive, and to guide the Children of Israel into victory. According to Psalm 23, David knows what it means to come away from battle, and have a feast with the Father. This becomes a place of peace and refuge, as God refreshes him for what lies ahead.

I have marveled at this psalm for years, as I think about God in the midst of the battle. He is not like us. We are afraid and wondering what the outcome will be. He is at peace, knowing that He is all-powerful and the enemy has to bow his knee. When we understand this aspect of God, it makes sense to take time and have a meal with Jesus, or to stop worrying about tomorrow, and rest at His feet, in prayer, knowing that He is in control. This is how we dine at His table, in the midst of the battle. The battle can be raging, but when we stop, we get a different perspective of our position, and we can see God's power and the victory we already have through Christ.

Taking a closer look at this psalm, we see it says, *"God prepares a table."* Even though we can see that David took the time, God, the Father, initiated the experience. He was the one who called and made the feast. It's the same with us. The Father wants relationship with us more that we want relationship with Him. God has sent us an invitation to dinner. Now we have to choose to come and dine with Him

One of the things we find hard to do when we have been the one who made mistakes, is to come and wait in the presence of God. The enemy will tell us that we're not welcome or worthy. Then we wrestle with our thoughts and feelings of guilt, wondering if the pain is worth the experience. However, if we just get through the moment and risk waiting on God, our wounds will start to heal. We can still bring our complaints about those who have wronged us to God, but once our hearts are still, we realize that God loves those who have judged us, the same that He loves us. Even though we want vengeance, God wants us to forgive. Those who have made mistakes, deserve the same response that God has given us, grace. This is how we let the invisible barriers down, that will allow our hearts to become soft again. What our accusers do is not our problem. They can only hurt us to the extent that we allow their words to undermine our position in Christ

I invite you to come and feast at the table of the King. Enjoy His presence and let Him do the talking. This will become a place of refuge, where the fear and stress of life will disappear, as we hear the plans that God has for us. He wants to speak into our hearts. The more time we spend with Him, the more we will hear His thoughts, and the less we will be controlled by our imagination.

The battle doesn't stop overnight, neither does the journey come to a quick conclusion. That is life. There is always something that's a challenge, In the midst of the season in which we struggle, we have to learn to do as God instructs, *"be still and know that I am God"*. If we never take time to have a relationship with God, we will not know Him in the midst of the battle, making the journey long and painful. If we still our hearts, and let God into our world during the battle, the journey may be just as long, but our hearts and attitudes will be different. Instead of us feeling like we are loosing everything, we will start seeing God's perspective. We will gain insight, and realize that even in our failures, we are victorious. What the devil meant for harm, God will turn for good. God teaches us valuable truths that will help us in our daily lives, and future ministry. By waiting, God is able to touch the hidden places of our heart, and we are able to touch the hearts of others.

Wait for the command to go!

Learning to "be still" to hear God's voice is one aspect of waiting. The other is, not stepping out to try and get back into ministry, before God releases you. I am sure we can all think back to the time we first entered the ministry, and the process of waiting before we were released. It seemed painful at times, and we wondered if the day would ever arrive. We thought we were ready, yet those around us thought it wise that we should wait. Their wisdom was right. I believe there is a right time for everything, and it's dangerous for us to step out when we think we are ready. We need to wait for God to open doors, or give the command. This is an area where people like to rebel. The fact is, that God has placed people in ministry to cover and protect. They are to speak into our lives, and God uses them to instruct us, or confirm when it's the right time to minister. There are some overpowering ministers that never want you to leave, but that is not true of all ministers.

If this was true when we first entered the ministry, it is also true in restoration. We have to prove ourselves again, and this begins in the local church. We need to learn to wait, and only start ministering when God releases us. It is not for us to open the doors, but we have to wait for God to open the doors. I never looked to start planting churches again, but God made it obvious when it was the right time, by sending the right people to speak into my life. I have seen ministers over the years, who have not dealt with the pain of their failure. They have ignored those around them, and placed themselves right back into the ministry. God, in His grace, continues to use them but they've never really healed completely, and they "walk with a limp." Their gift produces results, but if they had waited for God to release them, they would walk completely healed and the results of their ministry would be much greater.

Before Laura and I separated, God told me to resign, and step down from ministry, to receive restoration. At that moment, I felt God placed a time period of two years in my heart in which

I would be out of action. This proved to be the case. In fact, I forgot that God had given me this instruction and time period, until He reminded me of it when the first person came to me, and spoke about starting a new church. God is awesome! When I looked forward and thought about the time I would not be ministering, it was daunting, even scary. As I journeyed through the wilderness, there were times of fear and frustration. But now, I look back and I know that God was right. There are so many things He has worked in my heart, and I am better for it. I am glad that I had been hidden and isolated for that time to gain true healing.

In the New Testament, after Jesus' crucifixion and resurrection, Jesus visits the disciples on a number of occasions. Then, just before His ascension into heaven, He gives them one more instruction, *"Wait." (Acts 1:4)* They were to wait in Jerusalem, until they received the promise of the Holy Spirit. Their waiting and resting in God created a foundation for a blessed future. What would have happened to the church if the Apostles never waited for the outpouring of the Holy Spirit? They would still have a message, but the power would not have been there to accompany it! Being still, or waiting, was crucial for their future, and the future of the church.

They must have been excited. They had seen the resurrected Christ. They were buzzing and ready to tell the world. We see this when their desire was released on the day of Pentecost. The church exploded with salvation, people were healed, and incredible miracles took place! The environment that Jesus created by causing them to wait in Jerusalem, attributed to their explosive release. They had spent days praying and dreaming of what the future would look like, and when the day finally arrived, they couldn't hold back the gifts of God.

I often think that is what God does with us. We think we are ready to go and minister. However, when we wait for God's timing, the dream He placed in our heart has time to grow. When He releases us, the ministry is more explosive, and we achieve greater results. During the time of waiting, we may get frustrated because all we want to do is what God has called us to. We have tasted it before, and we think we are ready to do it again. We have to remember that we who have failed in one area of ministry, became lukewarm in our relationship with God. If this were not the case, we probably wouldn't have made the mistakes we did. So, in restoration, we need God to operate on us and set our hearts on fire again before He releases us back into ministry.

It's time for us to humble ourselves and place our lives back into the hands of God:

> *Likewise you younger people, submit yourselves to your elders, Yes, all of you be submissive to one another, and be clothed with humility, for, "God resists the proud, But gives grace to the humble" Therefore humble yourselves under the mighty hand of God, That He may exalt you in due time. Casting all your care upon Him, for He cares for you. Be sober, be vigilant; because your adversary the devil walks about like a roaring lion, seeking whom, he may devour. Resist him, steadfast in the faith, knowing the same sufferings are experienced by your brotherhood in the world. But may the God of all grace who called us to His eternal glory by Christ Jesus, after you have suffered a while, perfect, establish, strengthen and settle you. To Him be the glory and the dominion forever and ever. Amen (1 Peter 5:5-11)*

This scripture is rich with truth regarding our need to be still, and to trust that God is in control. Why do we need to humble ourselves? We have to realize the devil is a roaring lion. He wants to devour all believers, but especially those who are serving in ministry. The devil knows that God has a perfect plan and timing for everything. When we move with God, we experience His blessing. When we step out on our own, we open ourselves to the attacks of the enemy. We become a target like a zebra on the African plains that has wandered away from the pack. Isolated, she is vulnerable to the lion who wants his dinner!

Just as God wants us to humble ourselves, the enemy wants to create pride. The humble realize they can't do it on their own. The proud think they can do what they want, when they want. If the attitude of the humble is to "submit themselves under the hand of God," the attitude of the proud is to run on their own. God wants servant leaders, the enemy creates egotistical leaders. God wants to restore us and the enemy wants to deform us. He wants to get us running, and doing stuff on our own. We may be frustrated in the church during your time of restoration, but we humble ourselves. The enemy will whisper into our hearts and tell us that the church should be giving us more opportunities, or that it's time to do get on with the ministry, because he wants you in the open, away from the security of the church. If it's not God's time, and we step out on our own, doors won't open. We may make some kind of opening, but it will likely lead to failure and we will feel more hurt, rejected and wounded. When that happens, the enemy gets us where he wants us, and he can devour us.

Not only is the devil against us, but God "resists the proud". If we are to be successful in life or ministry, we need God with us, not against us. We need to learn the lessons God is teaching us in restoration. We may have been capable ministers before, but we had failed when we sinned. When we chose to get divorced, we operated in pride, driven by our self-will. We thought we could do it our way, and as a result, we have faced a wilderness ever since. Once forgiven, God wants to restore, but He can't release us back into ministry until we are humble. Disobedience creates sin, obedience creates favor. Once we have humbled ourselves, how long do we have to wait before we can get on with the ministry again? That time will differ for each person, but we will know the time because God "gives grace to the humble," and He "will exalt you in due time." When the time is right, God will promote us and open the doors.

God knows that we struggle with waiting. The scripture confirms this by declaring that we will "suffer for a while." However, during our "*suffering,*" we will be "*perfected, established, strengthened and set in place.*" When I think about restoration, and God's desire to release those who have fallen back into ministry, I see God's heart in making us better than we were before in our character and understanding. This process takes time and we have to humble ourselves and let God be God. The more we fight against this process the longer it takes! The sooner we submit, the more we learn, and the quicker we will be released back into ministry. God wants us ministering again. He gave us a gift that will bring an aspect of who He is into the lives of others, but he wants us ministering in the right way.

I learned a valuable lesson as a teenager in the church. I had heard the call of God and I was desperate to do all that God had called me to. I had been in the church for a couple of years, and helped in various areas of ministry. One of those areas was the church youth club. I was faithful to attend every Friday night and help set up equipment before it started and I helped put everything away when the service ended. I had preached in the youth services a number of times, and many of my peers came to share their struggles with me and ask for advice. The youth club was growing, and the church was thinking about making more people leaders, to help with the demand. I was sure that I would be made one of the new leaders. So, when they decided not to make anyone else a leader, I felt rejected, and I was angry. I decided I needed some answers, so I went to speak to the assistant pastor. He heard my complaint, and his response was not what I expected. I thought he would fight my cause, but instead he spoke wisdom. "Darren," he replied, "you are not a leader or a pastor because of a title, you are a leader because of your actions!" He was right, my pride wanted promotion and recognition for my gift, but a true leader will lead regardless of title or position. It was time to humble myself again and serve.

Consider Joseph and the journey he endured. His story starts in Genesis 37, at the age of seventeen. It is obvious to all his brothers that He is his father's favorite. He gets the best treatment and the best gifts. One of those gifts was a *"tunic of many colors."* Not only is he favored, he is also incredibly gifted. He is one of those people that find life easy, and they seem to have everything. But, Joseph had an issue with pride. He knew how much His father loved him, and the gifts he had. His heart was filled with the dreams that God had given him, but his expression was unwise and prideful. Joseph would take every opportunity he got to show off his gift to his brothers.

Unfortunately for Joseph, his pride created anger, and his brothers plotted against him. Joseph goes out to meet his brothers, and they take the opportunity to deal with him. First, they throw him in a pit. Then, they sell him to the Ishmaelite, and he ends up in Potiphar's house, and becomes very successful. In fact, too successful, in the eyes of Potiphar's wife. She falls in love with Joseph's charisma, and wants to sleep with him but he runs for his life. Then she speaks lies about him, and he ends up in prison. While he was in prison, he gained great favor and he is placed in charge over the other prisoners. It's during this time, that he hears that Pharaoh has a dream and no one can interpret it. With wise words, Joseph interprets the dream, speaking into the life of Pharaoh, and this leads to his release and eventual rise of power as he becomes the second in command over Egypt. (Genesis 37-50)

What a great story! What can we learn from this? Joseph's pride led to his downfall. But during the trials of his life, he learned to humble himself which changed his attitude and he became a servant. He didn't just do the right thing while people were watching, but when no one else was around. This is true integrity. What I like about Joseph is, that he ministered with the heart of God to all people, whether in prison or in a place of authority. He didn't just help people when he had the title, he gave his best all the time.

Joseph's attitude leaves us with a great challenge. If we are journeying through restoration, there is a time when we are not at the forefront of ministry, but we are hidden in the plans of God. What attitude will we exhibit? Will it be one of pride or will we demonstrate the heart of a humble servant. That's willingness to do whatever God desires. For those who are presently attending a church, and receiving restoration, they are there by God's grace. It's not always an easy process for the minister or the members of that church to stand by them in the midst of criticism they might be receiving. No matter how frustrated we get at not being in ministry at this time, they are not the reason for it. Show them great honor. It is an opportunity to humble ourselves, and do all that we can to help them. Remember, God is not looking at our title, or lack of it. God is looking at our hearts.

From wilderness to wilderness

There are many messages on the wilderness experience. The implication is that it's a season, or barren spell, that we have to get through. Then I read the following scripture:

> And the children of Israel set out from the wilderness of Sinai on their journey; then the cloud settled down in the wilderness of Paran (Numbers 10:12)

The Children of Israel went from wilderness to wilderness, or from one struggle to another, before they sent spies into the Promised Land. So, their wilderness wasn't because of rebellion or sin, it was just the journey they were on. It's the same for us. We often refer to the wilderness as a season or trial, but the fact is, that we journey from wilderness to wilderness before we come to the Promised Land. Through the time of restoration we go from trial to trial. There are many things that we will face, and to get through them, we will need to "be still". Take the time to dine with God, and get His perspective on the journey. We need to remain humble, place ourselves in the hands of God and he will exalt us when it is time.

"Blessed is the man whose strength is in You, Whose heart is set on pilgrimage (Journey). As they pass through the valley of Baca, (weeping) They make it a spring; The rain also covers it with pools (blessings). They go from strength to strength; Each one appears before God in Zion. (Psalm 84:5-6)

The process of restoration is a journey. We have fallen and made mistakes. The attitudes or desires that led to our sin did not develop overnight, and neither does restoration. The Holy Spirit needs to bring conviction not to the obvious sin, but to the underlying attitudes that led to us to make the choices we made. Once convicted, the process of rebuilding begins. It's a journey that some are not willing to travel, and others feel too weak and wounded to know how to begin. It's time for us to put our trust in God, setting our hearts on the journey ahead. It will be painful, and there will be many tears, but before long the tears will turn to joy and valley of weeping (Baca) will become a place of blessings.

I have written this book as one who has fallen, but I refused to lie down and play dead due to the lies and accusations of the devil. My transparency is to help others. Others need to know they are not alone in their pain, because in the midst of all the pain, God stands tall, as a shield against our accuser. His words are songs of grace. He is ever present, with arms opened wide, ready to embrace us as the father embraced the prodigal. He only waits for an invitation from us to begin this process of healing. Once we open the door of our hearts, God can reach out with the hands of the Creator, to take our broken vessel and start the process of remolding and restoring us into a vessel of honor.

Chapter 11
CALLING THE CHURCH

The process of restoration is not easy for the person being re-stored, or the church that's involved in the restoration. The prob-lem we face, is that every situation is different. How we see the "mess" that the fallen believer has created, determines how we respond. We are left with the question, "What would Jesus do"? This is something I have asked many times during my restoration, and yet, when I look at what Jesus would do, and what the church would do, I see two different pictures.

The image I have when looking at the life, ministry, and teaching of Jesus, it is full of grace. I see Jesus reaching out and embrac-ing those who are struggling. Then, I look at the church, and the picture is different. The church often struggles with restoration, not because people don't want to help, but because they don't know how to help. Fallen ministers and leaders are complicated. They should be examples of truth and righteous living and when they fail, churches are left feeling hurt and asking questions such as, "How did this happen"? The church often responds out of that hurt, and instead of reaching out with grace, it lashes out with judgmental words and uncaring responses.

The challenge we face is that we live in a world where people fail. Divorce is not right, and we should avoid it at all costs, but it still happens. Those who experience it, or other failures, are still God's children, whom He loves.

It's time for the church to look at their "W.W.J.D" wristbands and act accordingly. With that in mind, let's ask the question, "What would Jesus do" with the sinning saint in the church? The first thing we have to understand about Jesus is, that He placed Him-self in a nation of believers who were rebellious and doing their own things. He didn't come for the righteous, or the do-gooders. He came for the sinner, and the lost. Just think about the nation of Israel for a moment and the many times God spoke to them, called them, performed great miracles and delivered them from trouble. When we read the Old Testament and see the things God did for Israel, we are left wondering, "How they could have been so rebellious?" Most of what I read in the Old Testament about Israel, is how God deals with them in their rebellion, or the exile they find themselves in because of their sin. Yet, God continues to have mercy. Israel is no different than the church. In fact, in Acts 7:38, Israel is called "The church in the wilderness."

The first people Jesus reached out to were not the Gentiles, but the rebellious Children of Israel. Jesus said, *"I am not sent but unto the lost sheep of the house of Israel." (Matthew 15:24)*. This does not mean He was not sent for the rest of the world, but He came first to Israel. It was the job of the church that rose out of the church in Jerusalem (Israel) to reach the rest of the world. In saying this, I think the church is called to the "lost sheep" of our generation, or we can call them the "prodigal's in the church." In the parable Jesus told of the lost sheep, we see the heart of the Father, and the foundation in the ministry of Jesus:

> *Then all the tax collectors and the sinners drew near Him to hear Him. And the Pharisees and scribes complained, saying "This man receives sinners and eats with them". So He (Jesus) spoke this parable to them saying: "What man or you, having a hundred sheep, if he loses one of them, does not leave the ninety-nine in the wilderness, and go after the one which is lost until he finds it? And when he has found it, he lays it on his shoulders, rejoicing. And when he comes home, he calls together his friends and neighbors, saying to them, "Rejoice with me, for I have found my sheep which was lost!" I say to you there will be more joy in heaven over one sinner who repents than over ninety-nine just persons who need no repentance* (Luke 15:1-7)

In this parable, Jesus not only goes out of his way to find the lost sheep (sinner), but He places it on His shoulders until it is able to walk again. This is a clear picture of what Jesus would do with the sinning saints. He goes in search of them, and carries them. The church is too often like the Pharisees and scribes, who stand around moaning and questioning why Jesus would even spend time with the sinner. We have to conclude that it's the sinner that Jesus is called to. And whether that's an unbeliever, or sinning saint, Jesus will do all He can to bring restoration.

The next thing we need to realize, is that the first people that Jesus sent the disciples to were Israel:

> These twelve Jesus sent out and commanded them, saying "Do not go into the way of the Gentiles, and do not enter a city of Samaritans, but go rather to the lost sheep of the House of Israel" (Matthew 10:5-6)

Just as the rebellious children of Israel were the first people Jesus reached out to, they were also the first group that Jesus sent the disciples to. With that in mind, let's think about the church! Doesn't it make sense that the heart of Christ is to reach out to the believer that has fallen? Wouldn't we conclude that He has called us to reach out to the lost sheep of our generation? I can say with great confidence, God is calling the church to be a place of hope, security, love, and grace. We have not been called to reject our own, or trample on an already fallen believer. We have been called to do what Jesus would do, and that is to reach out to the fallen and bring restoration. Where does the church start with this process?

We need Fathers

Not everyone in the church has the grace or the gifting in leading the church in a ministry of restoration, but it needs to start somewhere. I believe the first people God calls to this ministry of reaching out to the fallen, are the fathers in the church, or should I say, those with a father's heart. The heart of a father is someone who never gives up on their children, no matter how much they mess up. The father always has hope that change will take place, or that the child will learn from their mistakes, and live a successful life.

The greatest picture we have of the father is in the parable of the prodigal son. We know the story of how the father allowed the son to make his own choices, even though he knew his son would mess up. And mess up he did...big time! We know the father was in great pain over the choices his son made, but it never stopped him from loving or looking out for him. When the son realized he had messed up, and decided to turn from his sin and go home, he thought he would only be good enough to take the place of a servant. He knew the extent of his mistakes, and he couldn't see past the judgment he felt he deserved for the mistakes he had made. (John 15:11-21)

The father's response however, was totally different from the son's expectation. While the son was a long way off, the father spotted him. He must have been looking out for him, as there was always a hope in his heart that one day his son would come home. Once he saw him, he turned into an Olympian sprint specialist, and got to him as quickly as he could! There was no anger, displeasure, shouting or look of disappointment in his eyes, just love! The joy the father felt was overwhelming. He couldn't keep himself from grabbing hold of him, and kissing him! He couldn't wait to get him home, to clothe him in the finest Israeli Gucci attire and throw him a big party. (John 15:20-23)

Now, the response we see from the brother, is bewilderment. He can't understand the grace of his father. He feels like an injustice has been done. He had never messed up like this! He had walked the line and done all the right things, yet he had never had a big party. Why? Where was his blessing? When he questioned the father, the father's response was, "You could have and can have this anytime you want, you just didn't ask." (John 15:27-32)

The problem we have in the church today is, that most of us are like the brother. We are all looking for the blessing and the rewards for doing the right things and walking a "Holy life." Then, when we see those who have messed up, receive grace and blessing, we think, "It's an injustice!" I have to agree, in human terms and human thinking, it seems wrong, and yet our display of jealousy, and anger is also sin. However, it's that very human reaction that distinguishes the heart of a brother, and the heart of a father. Brothers have an inability to see past their own emotions, thereby restricting them from ministering to the fallen brother. The heart of a father, sees through the eyes of love, and understands what the Heavenly Father desires, and reaches out in grace and love.

One of the reasons the church fails in the restoration ministry is because we have many pastors and leaders in the church, but we do not have many fathers:

> *"For though you might have ten thousand instructors in Christ, yet you do not have many fathers."* (I Corinthians 4:15a)

This is something that needs to change if we want our churches to become a place where restoration takes place. We need to pray, and ask God to give us a father's heart. It's no different than becoming a parent. We make a choice (most of the time) to have children, and once we have them, we fall in love with them. No matter how often they fall and make mistakes, or how many times we have to correct them, our love for them keeps us going. As time goes on, we get better at correcting them, and more importantly how we get better at exhibiting our love, even when they don't deserve it.

The ministry of restoration is not for the faint of heart. It can't be done in one day or a counseling session. It's a journey where two or more people learn to trust each other, creating an open and honest relationship for the process to begin. There has to be a commitment from both parties (the father and the fallen son), and an understanding that there will be times of disagreement, questioning and painful correction. There will also be times of hope, discovery and, at the right time, release back into ministry

Releasing the fathers heart in the church

Just because the church leader has a father's heart and a desire to see fallen ministers restored, it doesn't mean that the elders, leaders or church member share the same passion. This needs to change for a church to successfully minister restoration, or there will be conflict in the church, and it will lose people. I believe this was one of the problems in the first church that Amanda and I started going to. It was easy to see that the pastor of that church had compassion, and a desire to see us restored. That same passion was not felt by the elders that served with him, and in my opinion, they dictated his next move. This resulted in our feeling of rejected. We were left with no option but to leave the church.

The foundation for a restoration ministry starts with the church leaders, but it has to be shared by those who serve with them. The laying of this foundation does not start when a "sinning saint" comes into the church, it starts a long time before. It is the leader's responsibility to set the values of the church. Many churches are great at setting goals and understanding, "what" they are going to do. They are less successful at creating the right values in a church or in understanding "how," or with what attitude they are going to go about fulfilling the vision of the church.

It's important for the leaders in the church to discuss their values. What is it that they believe in? Do they believe in grace and compassion, and if so, what does that look like? Do they believe in bringing restoration to those who have sinned? Again, what does that look like? Is it something that is said, or is it part of the fiber and fabric of the church? Does it run through your veins and your thinking? Or is it just words that sound good from the pulpit? If grace and compassion are not part of the church's DNA, it has to be addressed at leadership level. Once the leadership understands this demonstration of the heart of God, it needs to be taught in the church. One of the things I am grateful for, is that in the church where we received restoration (Word of Life), the pastor was already teaching on the love of God before we arrived. Once we were there, it was part of the congregation's thinking, so now they had someone to practice on!

It's easy to show love to those who are lovely or clean. It's only God's grace that enables us to show love to those who are dirty! What did grace, compassion and the heart of restoration look like in the Word of Life Church? They welcomed us, but not our sin. They continued to walk with us, even when people in other churches spoke against us. They sat by us in church, and didn't leave us sitting in the back of the church on our own. They invited us to fellowship, and to share a meal. They encouraged us in due time to use and minister gifts we had, and were open to receiving the gifts we ministered. It was a word of encouragement, a hug when we were crying, and a willingness to take time to walk us through the mire of despair into a place of hope. This wasn't something that was just exhibited in Pastor Paul, but it was in the very life of the church. I believe the church did what Jesus would do. They reached out to the lepers (religious outcasts), embraced us, and allowed us to heal.

Ministering to the struggling

Once we have caught the heart of Jesus, and the desire to reach out to the lost sheep, the struggling saint, or the prodigals in the church, we have to ask ourselves, "How can we minister to them?" I wish I could give you a list of ten things to do with a promise of great results. Unfortunately, every situation is different, and the process of restoration varies with each individual. It depends on their willingness to progress, the areas they struggle to change, how much truth they grab hold of, or concepts they fail to grasp. It's a journey, not a formula! What we can look at is the attitude of the minister's heart. That is what's vital for restoration.

The first group we will look at are the struggling saints. Often before a person falls into sin, those around them can detect that there is a problem, or heart attitude that is not in alignment with the Word of God. The challenge is that we don't really want to believe that a minister may be struggling in an area of their life. So, those around them, often bury their head in the sand and hope the struggle will soon be resolved without interference. Rarely will they change on their own. The desire, wrong thinking or attitude can lead to greater imaginings and further wandering from truth. As a church, we have been called to be our brother's keeper, and we shouldn't be afraid of holding each other accountable for our Christian walk:

> Faithful are the wounds of a friend, But the kisses of the enemy are deceitful. (Proverbs 27:6)

Once we detect a problem, we need to approach the struggling couple or individual, and minister to them in truth and love. I include the word "love" for a reason. Often Christians discuss talking to a "brother or sister in love," but the words they use are far from the love of God. In fact, the church can be a very manipulative and judgmental place. Often our fear of what the individuals are struggling with, causes us to over react, and use language that accuses the struggling saint, rather than bringing them up to a place of understanding. It is words rooted in truth, and demonstrations of love that will help them in a way that Jesus would help them.

We must also understand that when we approach a person who is struggling, they may not see the situation like we do. There are many things about us that other people notice, that we do not. Sometimes, there is a period of time, when the saint is struggling with an issue, but they are in denial. They think they have their lives under control, and they are going to win the battle. Their response to our approach to minister may be defensive. Even though they act in a defensive manner, this doesn't mean that we need to respond with accusation. Instead, we need to endeavor to work with them, and bring them to a place of seeing truth.

The other challenge we face, is that some churches have a history of when they discover a person's struggles, they expose them before the church body. If a church has been quick to remove people from positions of leadership when they are struggling, this action is often taken due to fear or a power struggle. As ministers, we may be afraid of what the church congregation may think, if we do not deal with everything publicly.

The premise for this action is often taken from the book of Matthew:

> Moreover if your brother sins against you, go tell him his fault between you and him alone. If he hears you, you have gained your brother, But if he will not hear, take with you one or two more, that by the mouth of two or three witnesses every word may be established. And If he refuses to hear them, tell it to the church, but if he refuses even to hear the church, let him be to you like the heathen and tax collector!. (Matthew 18:15-17)

The church has often used this scripture to deal with a sinning saint. The "loving brother or sister" will go to the person who is struggling on several occasions, to point out their fault. If that a fellow believer doesn't respond, or change, the brother or sister feels justified in "taking it to the church." This usually means exposing the individual publicly, and then putting them out of the church.

What we need to understand about this scripture is, it refers to conflicts between brothers, more than individuals who have fallen in ministry. To put it in common day language, if we have a falling out with a friend, Joe, because he continues to lie to us, we call his attention to what he is doing. If he refuses to recognize it, we get someone else who will confirm what we are saying. If Joe still doesn't change, we take it to the church elders, and let them deal with him. If he still refuses to recognize his behavior, we are to treat him like we would treat someone in the world. We would not hang out together, but instead, get on with our lives and find other friends, at least till Joe changes his behavior. Put in this way, we see that there is no place in this scripture that says we should address a brother or sister's sin publicly, especially on a Sunday morning from the stage! It also does not say we are to put them out of the church, although that is how many have interpreted this portion of scripture.

We also need to read this in the context of gaining understanding of what would Jesus do. This scripture is sandwiched between the parable of the lost sheep and Jesus' response to Peter about forgiving a brother. Jesus encourages us to leave the ninety-nine sheep to find the one that's lost, (Matthew 18:10-14). In his discussion with Peter, regarding how often we are to forgive a brother's sin, Peter suggested seven times. Jesus, however, encourages him that he should forgive seventy times seven. (Matthew 18:21-22) So, unless we conclude that Jesus is contradicting Himself in how to deal with sin or a lost brother, we have to read this as a suggested way in which we are to deal with a brother who is struggling in an area of sin in his life.

When we look at the scripture in this manner, our approach changes. We should deal with the sin, one-on-one, and in a private environment. If they don't see their sin, we continue to try and reveal the error of their way, by bringing in another witness or two. Again, if they refuse to change, we bring it to the attention of the church. How we view the translation of the word "church," determines our next action. For me, the church spoken of here is not the place we meet on a Sunday morning. It is talking about those who have been given authority to decide matters, and maintain godly order in the church... the elders! I arrived at this conclusion by studying the church's actions in the Book of Acts. As we know, there arose a dispute in regards to the salvation of the Gentiles, and whether they should be circumcised. Some believers thought Paul was in error by not demanding circumcision, so the dispute was brought before the church in Jerusalem. This does not refer to the entire congregation, but it was discussed among the apostles and elders (Jerusalem Council) within the church, and they sorted out the problem and the solution. (Acts 15)

We also need to realize that in Matthew 18, when it says the believer who has refused the counsel of his brother (sister) is brought before the church, it doesn't describe how often, how many times or what process takes place between the "church" or the church elders and the sinning brother before the situation is resolved. The circumstances, and profile of the individual, will determine whether a public announcement will have to be made. This is something that is decided by the eldership. Considering the context of these verses, we have to remember that the heart of Jesus was to go in search of the lost sheep. He wants to bring the sinning brother to a place of restoration, and He wants us to have a heart that will forgive not seven times, but seventy times seven. There is a vast difference between the heart of man and the heart of God. Man is quick to point out a person's faults and expose them. But although the heart of God, is quick to convict a person's sin, He desires to cover the sinner in love and with grace, creating a safe environment in which to work in the heart of the believer.

A great example of this is found in Genesis. Noah, was the only righteous man God could find to build an ark. After the rains stopped, Noah became a farmer:

> And Noah began to be a farmer, and he planted a vineyard. Then he drank of the wine and was drunk, and became uncovered in his tent. And Ham the father of Canaan saw the nakedness of his father, and told his brothers outside. But Shem and Japheth took a garment, lay on both their shoulders, and went backwards and covered the nakedness of their father. Their faces were turned away, and they did not see their father's nakedness. So Noah woke from his wine and knew what his younger son had done to him.

> Then he said:
> Cursed be Cannan;

A servant of servants,
He shall be to his brethren,

And he said:

Blessed be the lord,
The God of Shem
And may Canaan be his servant.
May God enlarge Japheth
And may he dwell
In the tents of Shem;
And may Cannan be his servant".

And Noah lived after the flood three hundred and fifty years"
(Genesis 9:20-28)

When we read this scripture, we realize Noah had sinned, and his sin needed to be addressed, but not in the way Canaan went about it. As soon as he saw his father drunk, he wanted to tell his brothers and expose his father's sin. The result was that he was cursed. This has been the attitude of many in the church for years, and it's my belief, that we have brought a curse on the church rather than blessing. The heart of God is seen in the other two brothers, who wanted to cover their father and protect him. This brought them blessing.

The church needs to set an example of how to deal with people who are struggling, or those who have fallen. We should never turn a blind eye to those who are wrestling with sin, but we strive to do what Jesus would do. We need to speak the truth, but with an attitude of love. We need to create an environment in which people who make mistakes, can feel safe and be restored.

If the person who is struggling with sin, is in a place of authority or ministry within the church, and they refuse to change, the process becomes more difficult and they will eventually be asked to step down from their position of ministry for restoration to take place. I say this from a heart that always seeks restoration there are some that want to just remove a person so the church can move on. This is not the heart of God.

From my experience, I knew that the restoration I was going through, could not take place while I was still in ministry. Therefore, I resigned from my position of authority in the church, and submitted my life to Pastor Paul at Word of Life Church, in Bangor, Maine.

If the problem is detected early enough, and there is a positive response from the minister, the situation can be dealt with and the right protective measures can be put into place. This will produce checks and balances for the minister, and the church, so the minister can stay in position, and continue to minister in the church, working with those who have come along side him/ her. It is evident that there is no quick fix or easy answer when people in the congregation or the minister struggles with an area of sin. However, our heart should always be to bring truth and order, but it needs to be delivered with the heart of God, so that we love and protect the individual.

Dealing with the fallen minister

Our heart is no different when dealing with a minister, or leader, that has gone beyond the point of struggling, to committing a specific sin. However, in this situation, the starting position is different. God wants to show His love and grace, and He desires to protect them, but we are now dealing with someone who has made a choice, and walked in disobedience. Again, there is no specific method, or order in which things have to be done, but there are a number of key elements that are essential for full restoration of a leader to take place.

1.   *Fathers Heart*

The process of helping a fallen minister or leader in the journey of restoration, requires the lead minister of the church to have the "Fathers Heart." It's the heart of the father that looks for the lost sheep, or a lost son, and provides them with a safe environment in which healing can take place. Sometimes, this means we will go after those who we know have fallen, but other times, God will bring them to our church. Those who are in need of restoration, may be the culprit, or the victim. They will be feeling unworthy, unloved and like a leper (Mark 1). They feel they are viewed as outcasts by the church. They have come, despite the shame because they need God. Depending on their state of mind, and the condition of their heart, they may already know they can be restored, or they may be wondering if God still loves them. What they need is not a lecture about sin, but arms that are opened wide, ready and willing to embrace them. They need to know the church will accept them as they are, and that their brothers and sisters in Christ are willing to walk the journey with them.

2.   *Laying a honest foundation of truth*

Once the person knows they are loved, and that we, as a church, are willing to help them in their restoration, there needs to be laid a foundation of truth. There has to be honest, open conversation about what the person has gone through, or how they have fallen. Once we understand where they are at, we are able to minister truth from the Word of God, and discuss what God requires. However, in discussing these things, we have to understand that when the Bible speaks about right and wrong, it gives a perfect picture. For us, to get from one place to another, may be a journey.

Creating a foundation of truth will take time. There may be details that the individual will share straight away, but hold back other things for another time. They will also be looking for how we respond. If they are ministers, they know the truth of the Word, and they will have an expectation about what we will say to them. It is not so much the response they will be gauging, but rather, the attitude and the heart in which we speak the truth. We should never shy away from truth, but it must be ministered with the heart of the father. It was said of Jesus that He was *"full of grace and truth"*. *(John 1:14)*

3. Look for a repentant heart

Restoration is impossible without repentance, but repentance is more than shedding a few tears. Remember, the first tears a person sheds are not usually for the mistakes they have made, but because they have been caught! Their pride has been hurt, or they may have lost the ministry they had been involved in. As we continue to show unconditional love and speak truth, the barriers will come down, and their heart will become tender. The individual will start to understand what they have done wrong, and the pain they have caused others. One sign of repentance is when a person's feelings of sorrow change from being self-centered, to understanding how they have hurt others. Ultimate repentance will be evident when they accept the responsibility that they have rebelled against God, are truly sorry, and they desire to change their ways. The person's actions will provide evidence whether a change of heart has taken place.

Another thing we need to realize about repentance is, that it is not just dealing with obvious sin, like an affair, but it also involves the underlying heart attitude that initially led the person to the point of rebellion. Repentance doesn't happen overnight. It's a process of God putting His finger on areas of the person's life, the believer accepting His guidance which leads to the person changing. It sounds easy, but it's not. Most people don't like being told they are wrong, or admitting that they have made mistakes in more than one area of their lives. So, true repentance is more than one encounter, its many encounters.

4. Covering

The heart of the individual going through restoration is sensitive. They have made mistakes, they feel like an outcast and they have a bruised heart. Any amount of judgmental conversation, or people in the church attacking them, will further wound their heart and cause the process of restoration to take longer. They have made choices, and they will have to face the pain of their choices. As ministers in the church, we need to protect them. There will be people inside the church and from other churches who know about the individual's sin. Some people may want to expose them, and bring them down. These people may give advice on how they should be dealt with by the church. It's important to help the congregation have a loving attitude, and bring them to an understanding about God's grace and forgiveness.

It is difficult when we are dealing with people from other churches. It may be that they have come from the ministry of the fallen minister, and they feel let down. Again, we can only point them to the Word of God. There are some individuals who may come from a ministry that is less grace focused, displaying a more judgmental attitude about restoring a fallen minister. These are difficult people to convince, that what we are doing is godly. In fact, they may try to sway our opinions and attitudes toward the person being restored.

Once again, it is important that we act with a father's heart. We can listen to other's complaints and reasonings, but as a father, we cover and protect our children. I know that when I was going through my period of restoration, there were many people who came to Pastor Paul questioning what and how he was dealing with us. Not only did he speak truth into their lives, but he never told us at the time about those people who were coming to him. He was protecting us from their words, which he knew would have had a detrimental effect.

5.   Create Accountability

Accountability is something every Christian needs, whether they are in ministry or not. It is good to have people in our lives who will give us a spiritual check up and see how we are doing. This is an important part of being restored. When a person chooses to sin, they choose to follow their own counsel. They ignore the whispers of the Holy Spirit, and even some direct advice from people around them; because they think they have "it" under control. They discover that they don't!

Accountability means a person is able to give an account of their actions and take responsibility for how they are handling their situation. This is one way of understanding how the individual is progressing. It also enables us to see if they are following, or ignoring the godly counsel that is being given to them. Again, not everything we suggest will be right for them, and there may be some disagreements on the process. Some things we require, but the heart of both the restorer and the one being restored should be the same.

I believe that being accountable works both ways. We have the right to make requests of the person being restored and we are also responsible to follow up on the things we say we will do. One thing that is promised in most restoration situations is a meeting time. There is a need to get together for counsel and spiritual check-ups. In the beginning of the process, we are keen to do this as often as possible, but if the process takes longer than anticipated, we may be tempted to cancel a meeting or two. What does this say to the person that we are helping restore? It tells them that they are not as important as we once made them feel. Putting this into perspective, as time goes on, less meeting time is needed, but it's important that we expect accountability in the life of the person being restored. We need to show the same level of faithfulness to the things we have promised.

6.   *Communicate to the church.*

Communication is vital for the church if they are to understanding what's going on. It is not easy to do this in a productive way. We have to balance the confidentiality of the person being restored, and the curiosity of individuals in the congregation. Remember, they are all hearing the same things we are hearing about this person, and if the situation isn't dealt with correctly, we may lose some people. One of the things we have to understand is that it's impossible to bring restoration in a person's life, on our own. To be successful, we need the support of the elders, leaders and the congregation. When the person being restored has held a public position, such as a minister, they need to know that the pastor assisting in their restoration, may need to share some of what has happened with the elders, so they can understand and help support in the restoration plan. Put in a different way, sin happens in dark places and in dark corners of the heart. Restoration happens in the light with transparency. The things we cover, God uncovers. The things we uncover, God covers!

Once the elders are in agreement, the pastor needs to communicate with the leaders of the church. It's the leaders of the church that are really in touch with the rest of the congregation. They don't need to know the specific details, but they do need to know that restoration is taking place, and that counsel is being given. This information will filter through the church, assuring them that the issues are not being glossed over, and that the heart of Jesus is being demonstrated to the person being restored. Some individuals in the church will want more information. As supportive ministers, it's important that we communicate the process of restoration with the church members, but we don't have to give all the details. There will be times when we can talk in generalities from the pulpit, but this needs to be done at the right time, with the right heart and with input from those bringing restoration - the elders in the church and the one being restored.

7.   Public Repentance

Bringing the person being restored before the congregation to express their sorrow and repentance often seems like the logical first action needed. The problem with this is that we still are not really sure about the heart of the person. There may be tears because they are sorrowful, but that does not mean they are at the point of repentance. They may say the right things, but are they are not really heartfelt.

I believe it's better to start the process of restoration privately, and to work with the individual until they are in a better place. Then, the repentance is seen to be real by the fruit they have shown in the church. It may be necessary to say something from the pulpit, as a way of keeping people informed of the process, to communicate the heart of the ministry that is taking place. From my experience, I am thankful that I was not required to give a "tell all" to the church at the beginning of the process. I don't know if I would have been able to do this, or if I would have stayed around after being required to do this. After Amanda and I had been in the church for eighteen months, I expressed to the minister my desire to share our situation with the church. When I was given the opportunity, I was able to express true repentance. I was able to give a truthful report of the mistakes we had made, and a good report of the restoration God had brought us through. The church had witnessed the process we were going through, so on the day I shared with the church, the things that God had been doing in us, they rejoice with us. After I shared with the church, I laid a foundation for Pastor Paul to explain the journey he had gone through as he worked with us. This enabled him to answer some of the questions he was not willing to answer before, out of a desire to protect us.

8.   Seek outside Counsel

No matter how skilled a minister may be in helping a person through restoration, it is wise to seek outside help.

We can't do it on our own. The outside help may come from trusted elders within the church, or from other ministers outside the church. It's helpful to hear other perspectives and opinions of how to move things forward.

I also believe that restoration is best achieved, when there is a team of people working with the person being restored. They all bring a different aspect of truth and together they can best capture and understand the heart of God in this difficult process.

9.   Encourage participation

The person who has fallen usually wants to run and hide. They isolate themselves from society. Church is a hard place to come to as they feel they are on display, being watched, and to some degree they are. However, the isolation has to be broken so they can get connected with people again. What worked for me was the men's Bible study that took place during the day. I was invited and encouraged to join some of the men on Tuesday mornings at a local coffee house. The meeting was informal. The subject matter was dependent on what people felt that day, and everyone was encouraged to share. This was great for me, even though I held back much of the time. I began to share bits and pieces of what I knew from the Word of God. It was these meetings that gave me a real desire to get back into the Word. I believe that they were as important in my restoration as anything else I went through.

10.   Giving Opportunities to minister.

If the person being restored was once in ministry, then full restoration means being released back into ministry. Discerning the progress of the individual, the readiness of the church, and the amount in which we are willing to let them minister in the church, is a difficult balance but one we have to find. When we discern the time is right, give opportunities but make sure that they are gradual.

The person being restored may have great gifting that can help the church, and us but be aware that they have some character flaws. Avoid being too eager to release them, or to slow, because they will never be perfect. If you give an opportunity to the person being restored, make sure you meet with them, to see how they are doing and to discern what their heart attitude is, before giving them another opportunity to minister.

11. Evaluate progress

Evaluation is important in moving forward, but how do you evaluate the spiritual attitude of a person and where they are in the restoration process? There are several things we can look for, such as their accountability and whether they are doing the things we have requested. We can also look at their attitude toward the ministry. Are they supportive or divisive in their conversation with people in the church? What are they like in services? Are they entering in and worshiping, or do they look like they have come to a funeral?

12. *Release at the right time*

There is always the right time to release a person back into ministry. Only those who have walked with the individual through the restoration process really know when this time is. We need to be sure it's not our timing or theirs, but that it's God who is opening the doors, and calling them back into ministry. The important thing is that restoration should be a thorough process. We are digging up the old foundation, and laying down a new foundation on which they will be able to stand for the rest of their life and ministry. God has not finished with them; He has just started a new work!

Final Thoughts To the Reader

I want to thank you for taking the brave step of picking up this book, and traveling with me on the road of my restoration. I hope you have gleaned something from it. It's my prayer that there has been moments of truth when the lights were turned on, and the Father connected something in your heart, which has helped you move forward in your restoration. I want to finish by sharing an experience I had at the time of writing the final chapter of this book.

Amanda and I had decided to take the children on a long weekend to one of our favorite places, New York City.

During one of the days we were there, we realized that the things that a fifteen-year-old girl (or should I say young woman) wants to do are very different from the things a seven-year-old boy wants to do. So, we decided that Amanda would spend some time with Katelynn, at the wax museum, and that Connor and I would go to Central Park to visit the zoo! After a few days in Times Square among all the people, Connor was pleased to get to the park and play. The first thing he saw were the massive rocks, and like any boy, he wanted to climb to the top of them. I guess the childlike feelings were still alive in me, because I wanted to do the same! I chased after him, laughing, climbing, taking pictures and having a blast.

In the midst of the fun, Connor heard my constant reminder, "take it slow, don't run, the rocks are slippery, just take your time". It's fair to say I was enjoying this adventure as much as he was. I wanted to be the hero, the model parent, and create fun and safety all at the same time. Then it happened. With a camera in one hand, and Connor's pretzel in the other, I moved too fast. My feet slipped out from under me and I landed on my back, looking at the sky! As beautiful as the Manhattan skyline is, I never wanted to look at it from this position!

Pain paralyzed my movements for a second, and Connor looked down at me with panic. In that moment, all I want to do is cry as I thought about the real pain and the humiliation of others watching! I had a choice. Do I lie there or get up? I got up, brushed myself off and laughed about my fall. In that moment, I decided that I wouldn't allow the pain in my back, or the blood dripping down my arm, to stop the fun we were having. I carried on running and carrying Connor on my shoulders, and having a good time.

The next day, I woke up feeling a little stiff. I was still scared from my fall, and even though the pain was real, there was something else on my mind. I had first visited New York City ten years before, and fallen in love with the place. I take every opportunity presented, to go back. When I'm in the city, I take time to run through Central Park. I had always had the desire to run the entire perimeter of the park, but I had never had the time. On this particular day, I did.

Again, I faced a moment of choice. The pain in my back was still there, but my dream was just in front of me. I decided to do the run. I left the hotel in Times Square, ran to the park, completely around its perimeter, enjoying seeing the houses, churches, museums and arrived back at the hotel. As I was about to complete the run, I heard the Holy Spirit speak into my heart and say, "Darren, dare to dream!" I knew in that moment that the Holy Spirit was telling me that the past was behind me, and that He was allowing and creating dreams in my heart again for the purpose of the kingdom of God

One day, I failed to listen to my own advice and found myself fallen, looking up at the sky. The next day, I ignored the scars and pain from my fall, and fulfilled a dream I had had for years, and finished the run that was before me. In life, we will all fall and find ourselves looking up. In that moment, we have the choice, to stay there or get up and run. What will you choose to do?

For more information

You can find all our current information and details about ministry on the web:

www.thesanctuarychurch.us

www.cre8consultancy.org

Please contact us if:

- If you are in need of restoration.

- If the book has helped you and you would like to testify.

- If you would like Pastors Darren and Amanda Farmer to minister in your church

- If you are setting up a program of restoration for an individual or couple and would like some support in the process.

- If you would like to network with us in creating a place of restoration in your area

45257678R00117

Made in the USA
San Bernardino, CA
04 February 2017